ECONOMIC RESEARCH CENTRE

REPORT OF THE
NINETY-SIXTH ROUND TABLE
ON TRANSPORT ECONOMICS

held in Paris on 10th-11th June 1993
on the following topic:

SHORT-DISTANCE
PASSENGER TRAVEL

EUROPEAN CONFERENCE OF MINISTERS OF TRANSPORT

THE EUROPEAN CONFERENCE
OF MINISTERS OF TRANSPORT (ECMT)

The European Conference of Ministers of Transport (ECMT) is an inter-governmental organisation established by a Protocol signed in Brussels on 17th October 1953. The Council of the Conference comprises the Ministers of Transport of 31 European countries.[1] The work of the Council of Ministers is prepared by a Committee of Deputies.

The purposes of the Conference are:

a) to take whatever measures may be necessary to achieve, at general or regional level, the most efficient use and rational development of European inland transport of international importance;

b) to co-ordinate and promote the activities of international organisations concerned with European inland transport, taking into account the work of supranational authorities in this field.

The matters generally studied by ECMT – and on which the Ministers take decisions – include: the general lines of transport policy; investment in the sector; infrastructural needs; specific aspects of the development of rail, road and inland waterways transport; combined transport issues; urban travel; road safety and traffic rules, signs and signals; access to transport for people with mobility problems. Other subjects now being examined in depth are: the future applications of new technologies, protection of the environment, and the integration of the East European countries in the European transport market. Statistical analyses of trends in traffic and investment are published each year, thus throwing light on the prevailing economic situation.

The ECMT organises Round Tables and Symposia. Their conclusions are considered by the competent organs of the Conference, under the authority of the Committee of Deputies, so that the latter may formulate proposals for policy decisions to be submitted to the Ministers.

The ECMT Documentation Centre maintains the TRANSDOC database, which can be accessed on-line via the telecommunications network.

For administrative purposes, the ECMT Secretariat is attached to the Secretariat of the Organisation for Economic Co-operation and Development (OECD).

---

1. Austria, Belgium, Bosnia-Herzegovina, Bulgaria, Croatia, the Czech Republic, Denmark, Estonia, Finland, France, Germany, Greece, Hungary, Ireland, Italy, Latvia, Lithuania, Luxembourg, Moldova, the Netherlands, Norway, Poland, Portugal, Romania, the Slovak Republic, Slovenia, Spain, Sweden, Switzerland, Turkey and the United Kingdom. (Associate Member countries: Australia, Canada, Japan, New Zealand, the Russian Federation and the United States. Observer countries: Albania, Morocco.)

Publié en français sous le titre :

LES DÉPLACEMENTS DE PERSONNES
A COURTE DISTANCE

TABLE RONDE 96

TABLE OF CONTENTS

GERMANY

Werner BRÖG
Erhard ERL

SOCIALDATA
Munich
Germany

THE IMPORTANCE OF NON-MOTORISED TRANSPORT FOR MOBILITY IN OUR CITIES

SUMMARY

Munich, January 1993

8

1. INTRODUCTION

The beginning of reconstruction after the Second World War meant, among other things, new bases and objectives for transport policy and planning. Attention was mainly directed at the promotion of motorised private transport, which was resolutely and systematically pursued, even where this led to disadvantages for the other transport modes.

Non-motorised transport was particularly hard hit, mobility in many planning concepts being reduced to motorised mobility, even though the proportion of non-motorised mobility amounted to at least half of all trips until the early seventies. This led to judgments and assessments of mobility which, even though mistaken, became widely accepted guidelines for transport planning.

This hitherto stable structure was shaken slightly for the first time at the beginning of the eighties with the rediscovery of the bicycle. Despite considerable efforts however it has still not been possible to make the bicycle generally recognised as an everyday mode of transport.

When it finally became clear at the beginning of the nineties that the promotion of motorised private transport is simply not capable of resolving the associated problems itself, even the automobile industry, for example, admitted that transport planning based on a single mode just cannot work.

However, since the earlier fixation of the mobility concept on motorised mobility was, for the most part, not abandoned, the promotion of public transport and its linking with motorised private transport was seen as the only measure that could improve transport conditions in our towns. This view was based on the earlier misjudgments on (motorised) mobility, which are still very prevalent.

These misjudgments are largely responsible for the fact that the importance of non-motorised transport for an effective, and acceptable, mobility system in our towns continues to be underestimated.

For this reason, we have endeavoured to bring together certain important aspects of mobility in our towns and to highlight the importance of the non-motorised modes.

The greater part of the data presented in this study is based on surveys carried out in fourteen (West) German towns over the period 1989 to 1991. These are referred to by the term "Conurbations 90". These surveys were carried out among people of all age groups for all week days.

2. MODAL CHOICE

On an average weekday, the residents of the fourteen towns covered by this study make a good quarter (26 per cent) of all their trips on foot and a further tenth by bicycle. Non-motorised transport thus amounts to 36 per cent of all trips. Together with the 14 per cent covered by urban public transport, this means that precisely 50 per cent of all trips use what are known as the environment-friendly modes (Figure 1).

Motorised private transport is used for the other half of the trips. By far the greater share falls to car drivers (38 per cent), followed a long way behind by car passengers (11 per cent), with only one in a hundred trips being made by motorised two-wheeler (moped, motorcycle).

A comparison of the individual towns reveals regularities and differences in non-motorised transport: while the proportion of trips made on foot lies round about the 25 per cent mark, the bicycle share ranges between 1 per cent in Wuppertal and 22 per cent in Bremen.

The form in which modal choice has been shown in Figure 1 (according to the "main mode") is very commonly used these days in behaviour-oriented studies. In transport planning, on the other hand, the so-called modal split is very often still used. Here, non-motorised transport is not taken into account and the three motorised private transport modes are added together into a "private transport" value and considered in relation to the "public transport" modes (Figure 2).

This latter representation is not only incomplete (since as a rule it ignores a good third of total mobility), but it is also misleading. Thus, for example, the 30 per cent share for car driver trips in Bremen leads to a private transport share of 70 per cent of modal split and, for example, in Gladbeck the private transport share of modal split is higher than in Bochum (88 as against 85 per cent) even though the proportion of car driver trips is significantly lower (39 as against 45 per cent).

2.1. Representation of modal choice

The two forms shown are by no means the only ways of representing modal choice (Figure 3).

Overall, the fourteen towns considered average 2.9 trips per person per day. For each of these trips however an average of 1.56 transport modes are used. Here trips on foot account for by far the greatest proportion (78 per cent), whereas the modal combinations "bike and ride" and "park and ride" play scarcely any role (0 = less than 0.5 per cent).

A breakdown of car passengers shows that about one quarter are not from the same household as the driver, but from another; a breakdown of the public transport modes shows that bus and rail-based systems have roughly equal shares.

The representation according to the "main mode" reduces the public transport share (bus and rail together) and, above all, trips on foot (the distances covered on foot when using other modes being ignored, though the trips made solely on foot remain). All the other methods of representing modal choice are based on determining the main mode.

In the case of the "modal traffic light", the drivers of cars and motorised two-wheelers are lumped together and the environment-friendly modes (foot, bicycle and public transport) are also summed. In the "extended modal split", the non-motorised modes (foot and bicycle) are summed, as are the motorised private modes (motorised two-wheelers, car drivers and car passengers).

On the other hand, with the "modal split", which disregards non-motorised transport, the number of trips (per person per day) falls from 2.9 to 1.9. Modal split is also frequently represented on the basis of the relative distances covered, which further increases the private transport share (from 78 to 82 per cent).

The breakdown of the main mode according to distance also shows the dominance of the car driver whereas a comparable representation on the basis of the time spent using each mode shows that the non-motorised modes dominate.

11

A completely different method of representing modal choice is "participation", which shows the proportion of persons who on an average day use a given transport mode at least once. The participation values add up to 136 per cent which means an average of 1.36 (most used) modes per day per mobile person (i.e. persons who leave the dwelling at some time during the day).

2.2. Estimation of modal choice

The proportion of trips made entirely on foot in our German towns, on average about one quarter, is very much underestimated by the residents. In Hamburg, where the actual value is in fact relatively low at 22 per cent, the residents estimate it at only 9 per cent; in Wismar, which has the peak value of 45 per cent, the estimate rises to 20 per cent, but in both towns the estimate is almost the same in relative terms (being somewhat over 40 per cent of the actual value). On the other hand, the proportion of public transport and, above all, motorised private transport, is significantly overestimated (Figure 4).

These estimates reflect a general opinion greatly influenced by experts and opinionmakers (Figure 5). A study in the Ruhr corridor shows, for example, that even the transport planners very greatly underestimate the proportion of trips made on foot (10 per cent instead of the actual 28). The example from Graz confirms that shopkeepers greatly underestimate the proportion of their own customers coming on foot and overestimate that of car users. The reason given for the (assumed) high proportion of customers using the car to go shopping is very often that of the problem of carrying the goods. However, one of the few studies concerned with this question came up with quite different findings: well over a third (38 per cent) of all purchases in the centre of Graz gave rise to no "transport requirement" and in well over half (58 per cent) a bag was carried. Bigger or unusual objects (e.g. prams) were found in only one in 25 cases. Here car drivers had the smallest and cyclists and pedestrians the greatest "transport output" (Figure 6).

An important reason for erroneous estimates of modal choice by opinionmakers is certainly their own behaviour (Figure 7). A breakdown of modal choice according to the "traffic light" method shows that the proportion of car drivers is dominant only in the case of employed males. This group represents only about one-quarter of the population, but at least three-quarters of the opinionmakers belong to it.

12

2.3. Spatial distribution

A further misjudgment often found concerns the spatial distribution of mobility. Here it is often forgotten that by far the greater proportion of all trips made by urban dwellers do not go beyond the city limits. In fact, five out of every six trips remain entirely within the home town. For a further seventh (14 per cent) the trip begins in the home town and ends elsewhere or begins elsewhere and ends in the home town (so-called outgoing/incoming trips). Only 3 per cent of all trips begin and end outside the home town (Figure 8).

The proportion of non-motorised transport increases significantly in the case of trips entirely within the home town, notably at the expense of car driver trips (Figure 9).

Within the towns there are areas in which non-motorised transport is clearly dominant. Thus, for example, 70 per cent of trips in the city centres are made on foot and a further 7 per cent by bicycle (Figure 10). The proportion of motorised private transport falls to 16 per cent and that of car drivers to about one-tenth. Here, however, there are substantial differences between the fourteen towns, differences which reflect not least the planning philosophy of the particular town concerned.

3. MOBILITY

Modal choice is one of the indicators we use to describe the type and structure of our mobility. In order to understand modal choice we therefore also need to understand mobility: here certain mobility parameters are useful.

3.1. Duration of travel

Since the studies by Zahavi, it has been known that travel time per person per day varies around the one hour mark. This is the case in our fourteen towns (Figure 11): the actual values range between 54 and 74 minutes, with the average being exactly one hour.

If this hour is divided up among the different transport modes (on the basis of all modes used), it can be seen that the biggest individual share goes to the foot mode and almost half to the non-motorised modes as a whole (Figure 12).

Even in the case of car trips and trips made by public transport, a certain amount of walking is involved, which makes up one-seventh of the total (door-to-door) journey time for a car trip and about one-quarter in the case of public transport (Figure 13).

If all the walking involved in the use of other modes is added to trips made solely on foot, the average inhabitant of our fourteen towns (of all age groups) covers a distance of 481 kilometres a year on foot and spends a total of 140 hours walking (Figure 14). If we add to this the 360 kilometres per person per year covered by bicycle, then the average inhabitant spends just half an hour a day using the non-motorised modes, covering 841 kilometres a year in this way.

3.2. Activities

Mobility is not an end in itself, but as a rule serves for the exercise of activities. The (away from home) activity programme for most people is relatively simple: whoever leaves the house as a rule exercises about two activities a day. Since only a little over three-quarters of urban dwellers leave home on an average day, the number of activities per person per day ranges between 1.4 and 1.9 (Figure 15).

A good four-fifths of the destinations at which these activities are carried out are reached direct from home. Three-quarters of all purchases are made within a radius of not more than three kilometres and two-thirds of all leisure activities are within no more than five kilometres of home. Two-thirds of all schools are also found within this radius. On the other hand, one in every three work places is more than ten kilometres from home (Figure 16).

3.3. Distances

The average person makes about 1 000 trips a year, or roughly three trips per day (Figure 17).

If these trips are broken down according to the distance covered, then the picture is fairly uniform no matter what the structure of the town: roughly one-quarter of all trips are of no more than one kilometre, roughly half no more than three kilometres; about two-thirds remain within a radius of five kilometres and five-sixths are no more than ten kilometres (Figure 18). In the case of trips entirely within the town the radii are even smaller: almost one-third of these trips are within one kilometre and another third between one and three kilometres (Figure 19).

3.4. Trend over time

Over the past fifteen years, the proportion of trips on foot (as the most used mode) has fallen from 36 to 26 per cent, or by over one-quarter. There has also been a decline in motorised two-wheelers, car passengers and public transport whereas the proportion of cyclists and car drivers has significantly increased, by a good 40 per cent in each case (Figure 20).

The enormous increase in car driver trips has had no effect on mobility, however: despite considerably higher car availability, the number of activities and trips have remained constant. The travel time too has remained unchanged and only the distance covered has increased, by three kilometres a day (Figure 21).

This increase in distance can also be seen in a breakdown according to distance covered. The proportion of trips up to and including three kilometres has fallen from 53 to 52 per cent (trips of up to one kilometre fell from 29 to 25 per cent while trips of from one to three kilometres increased from 24 to 27 per cent), while trips of over three kilometres increased from 47 to 48 per cent (three to five kilometres remaining the same at 15 per cent and over five kilometres rising from 32 to 33 per cent).

It can also be seen that the proportion of trips on foot in the short-distance category has fallen by a quarter (from 32 to 24 per cent); this fall led to an increase in bicycle and car trips by three percentage points each (Figure 22). In the case of trips of more than three kilometres, only the car driver share increased, at the expense of all other transport modes other than the bicycle.

A breakdown according to four simple socio-demographic groups (Figure 23) gives a good picture of where the increase in car driver trips has occurred: in the case of the over-sixties (from 14 to 24 per cent, up by three-quarters) and women (24 to 39 per cent, up by just two-thirds).

3.5. Car use

With short overall distances in everyday mobility, the distances covered by car must also be fairly short: of all car trips made by the residents of the fourteen towns, 7 per cent are already completed within one kilometre, almost one-third within three, just one half within five kilometres; almost three-quarters of all car trips are of no more than ten kilometres and only one in fifty is to a destination more than fifty kilometres from the starting point. Again the differences between the towns are fairly small (Figure 24).

The (door-to-door) speeds achieved by car are also rather low: over the average walking distance (1.1 km) the speed of the 8 per cent of all car trips up to this distance is 6 kph (as against 4 kph on foot). Anyone driving over this distance therefore saves just four minutes as compared with a pedestrian. The difference between the car and the bicycle is even less (two minutes' time saving with the car over the average bicycle trip distance). Lastly, the 73 per cent of car trips which are within the radius of the average public transport trip reach a speed of 18 kph (as against a public transport speed of 15 kph) and a time saving of six minutes (Figure 25).

4. REPLACEMENT OF CAR TRIPS

The present traffic situation is marked by the strong dominance of motorised private transport. The consequences of this dominance for man, the environment and the town are so serious that at present many possibilities for reducing car traffic are being considered. In this connection, however, it is also necessary to examine the extent to which greater promotion of each individual alternative mode could lead to the replacement of car trips. This is, at present, the focus of attention in urban transport.

4.1. Replaceability of car trips

A (private) car registered in one of our fourteen towns is used for an average 889 trips per year; by far the greater part of these trips (651 or roughly three-quarters) remain within the city limits. If these trips are broken down according to distance and purpose, the resulting matrix is as shown in Figure 26. It turns out that (in trips entirely within the town) every tenth car trip is completed within one kilometre and is of an average distance of 800 metres. A good quarter (29 per cent) are to a destination within one and three kilometres and almost a quarter (22 per cent) between three and five kilometres (the average distance being 2.4 and 4.4 kilometres, respectively).

16

The most important trip purposes are (with almost equal shares of a good quarter each) work, leisure and shopping (including the use of services such as post office, doctor, etc.).

Even a superficial glance at the individual fields of the matrix shows that there are clearly a good many car trips for which it is difficult to imagine that it is absolutely necessary to use the car.

For a closer examination of the possibilities for replacing car trips it is necessary to test for each individual trip whether there was an objective reason for car use (e.g. business use of the car, car trip within a longer transport chain, transport problems, etc.) and whether an alternative mode would in fact have been available.

In the case of car trips with no objective reason for car use and with at least one alternative mode there must obviously be only subjective reasons deciding the modal choice. In the survey towns, the proportion of such trips is 60 per cent of the total (Figure 27). Thus, if a total car ban were imposed in our towns, almost two-thirds of the motorists would have no great problem in still reaching their destinations.

In the following discussion we examine only the environment-friendly modes (foot, bicycle, public transport) as alternatives to the car, not the possibility of car-pooling. It turns out that public transport would certainly have the biggest substitution effect (33 per cent of all car trips within the town could immediately be taken over by public transport modes without any substantial system improvement in public transport), but that the importance of the bicycle is only slightly less (30 per cent) and almost one-fifth (19 per cent) of all car trips (within the town) could be replaced at any time by walking (Figure 28).

4.2. Non-motorised transport modes as alternatives to the car

Of the 651 trips within the town per (private) car per year, 392 are in principle already substitutable today; in the case of almost half these trips (195) a switch to the bicycle would be possible.

If we assume that in the case of these car trips from which there could in principle be a modal switch, the switch actually takes place in every fourth case, then 49 trips per year would be replaced by the bicycle (i.e. roughly four trips a month). Such a, very moderate, behavioural change would already increase bicycle use by one-fifth (Figure 29).

If we assume that the substitution of walking for car trips actually took place in every second possible case, then a further 22 car trips a year would be eliminated and the proportion of trips on foot would increase by 12 per cent (Figure 30).

These behavioural changes would already switch 111 car trips (roughly two trips a week) to other modes and thus reduce the proportion of car trips in total trips within the town by a sixth (17 per cent). This would be achieved with only something over one-quarter (28 per cent) of the theoretically substitutable car trips being actually switched to other modes (Figure 31).

4.3. The potential for non-motorised transport

Almost every third car trip entirely within one of the fourteen towns (30 per cent) could in principle be replaced by cycling (see Figure 28). This means that there is no objective reason for car use and that a bicycle is actually available.

In order to examine the question as to under what conditions the theoretically possible modal switch will actually be made, an analysis model using the so-called situation approach was used. With this method, the external and internal framework conditions for modal choice (subjective behavioural situation) was determined in detail for each individual trip. From these subjective behaviour situations it is then possible to derive the potential for measures. The aim of these measures must be to put the person concerned in a situation of external and subjective freedom of choice between car and bicycle in the case of a concrete trip. This does not mean that there will actually be a modal switch, but rather that a switch is possible at any given moment.

The potential analysis shows that already today -- without any further planning measures -- there is freedom of choice with respect to the bicycle in one-quarter of the potentially substitutable car trips. The assumptions of Figure 29 could thus already be fulfilled if only the free choice (with respect to the bicycle) car trips switched mode.

Taken as further potential fields were the (subjectively perceived) effects of journey time, transport quality of the infrastructure and travel comfort. Here, it turns out that measures in all three fields have a potential for influencing one-eighth to one-sixth of the (available) car trips. Long-known findings are confirmed here: purely planning measures in the field of bicycle infrastructures have only a relatively small potential. A substantial increase in this potential would be possible, however, if the general opinion regarding the bicycle as an

18

everyday transport mode in the towns were improved: the situation group "community climate" covers almost one-third of the car trips considered here (Figure 32).

A comparable consideration for car trips substitutable by walking gives similar results. The proportion of free-choice trips today is already nearly half (45 per cent); here again, therefore, the assumptions of Figure 30 are (almost) already fulfilled, even if only the free-choice car trips switch modes. Here again also, the potential group "community climate" is very much more strongly occupied (20 per cent) than the potential group "infrastructure" (9 per cent) and here again measures in the system ("hard policies") only have lasting success if they are accompanied by suitable measures for the head ("soft policies") (Figure 33).

5. OPINIONS AND EXPECTATIONS

Transport planning and policy over several decades was characterised by attempts to promote motorised individual transport even where this led to disadvantages for public transport and the non-motorised modes. For a long time this strategy enjoyed broad support among the population.

Towards the end of the eighties and in the early nineties, however, this view began to change significantly. The reasons for the change were increasing concern for the weaker road users and pedestrians and growing awareness of the threat to the town and the environment posed by motorised private transport. In both cases, the non-motorised modes play a special role: their users are particularly threatened by motorised private traffic and they offer easily usable alternatives to car use.

A survey in the European Community countries shows that over half (56 per cent) of EC citizens consider the risk of being involved in a road accident as a pedestrian to be (very) high; the corresponding estimation of the risk for cyclists is as high as almost three-quarters (70 per cent). Here there are very substantial differences between the individual countries (Figures 34, 35).

Not least for these reasons, town-dwellers want transport planners and policymakers to switch from favouring motorised private transport to giving priority to the environment-friendly modes (Figures 36, 37): in the opinion of three-quarters (73 per cent) of EC citizens, in the case of any conflict arising in

19

traffic planning, priority should be given to the bicycle, even when this leads to disadvantages for car traffic. Even more marked (85 per cent) is the desire for preferential treatment for pedestrians.

In this wish for a new orientation of transport policy and traffic planning, the citizens of the EC countries do not differ from their (local) political representatives (Figure 38). It is therefore surprising that the change in transport planning -- obviously desired on all sides -- is being introduced so hesitantly. The answer to this question can be, somewhat exaggeratedly, described as a "reciprocal mental block" between residents and decisionmakers. Decisionmakers in fact underestimate the actual opinion among the population just as much as the residents underestimate that of the (policy) decisionmakers (Figures 39, 40).

In this situation, each city centre is emotionally a particularly favourable crystallisation point for beginning a transport policy change. Four out of five residents in the conurbations of the "former" Federal Republic of Germany, for example, welcome the concept of the "low car" inner city, three-quarters of them (76 per cent) also in their own place of residence (access by car only for residents, delivery traffic and with special authorisation). The reasons given are particularly interesting: first comes the expectation of better shopping conditions, followed by the hope for improvement in environmental quality and road safety (Figure 41).

Despite the hopes and expectations of a change in transport policy, motorised private transport still makes an overwhelming impression on both citizens and decisionmakers: nearly all the car use indicators are very greatly overestimated -- in people's heads, the contribution that the (private) car makes to everyday mobility is at least twice as great as it is in fact! (Figure 42).

6. FURTHER CONSIDERATIONS

Through the example of non-motorised transport, three "syndromes" which are still interfering with transport planning can be seen very clearly.

a)   The "active traffic participation syndrome"

Traffic planning is traditionally concerned with the part of our lives in which we actively participate in traffic. On average we spend one hour a day travelling (see also Figure 21), i.e. about 4 per cent of our lives. During the remaining

23 hours we do not actively participate in traffic, but are nevertheless subjected to the consequences of the active participation of others (passive participation).

Traffic planning efforts, however, are as a rule concerned with organising traffic participation for the active instead of being mainly concerned with making active transport participation as bearable as possible for the passive participants.

Radical rethinking in this area would immediately make it clear that in the case of a substantial proportion of the trips in our towns it is simply not acceptable that they should be covered by car and that there are preferable alternatives using non-motorised modes.

b) The "measures/actionism syndrome"

Traffic planners and transport policymakers are convinced that changes in behaviour in the field of mobility can only be brought about through "hard measures" (in the system).

At the same time, it has long been known that we all perceive our environment (i.c. also systems) subjectively, that the resulting subjective worlds are certainly incomplete and distorted -- and yet it is precisely these that determine our behaviour -- and that changes in the subjective worlds can have just about as much behavioural change effect as measures affecting the system.

Thus, for example, in the case of 60 per cent of car trips entirely within the towns examined here, there is already today at least one alternative of more or less the same value (see Figure 27). For 19 per cent of these trips the city dweller could just as well go on foot (see Figure 28). In the case of almost half of this 19 per cent, all that is lacking is personal will (free choice), while for a further fifth there is the feeling that as pedestrians they will be looked down upon (community climate) and this is the reason for choosing the car (see Figure 33).

If we take only these two subsectors of car trips which could in principle be replaced by walking, this would represent 81 trips per car per year. In a town with 500 000 inhabitants and 250 000 private cars, these 81 trips per car would amount to a total of some 20 million trips a year, or about 55 000 trips a day.

As compared with this, building multi-storey car parks on the outskirts of the town as recommended by the automobile industry at present would probably provide parking for 3 000 cars. This would result in a reduction of about 7 000 car trips within the town, or just one-eighth of the reduction potential mentioned above. Even if we also assume that the distance of the 7 000 saved trips is four times as long, then the traffic relief effect of switching to walking is still twice as great.

However, in the one case there would be a construction cost of at least DM 50 million, while in the other only a small fraction of this sum would be required for a "communicative" programme to convince people, and a few modest supporting planning measures would suffice.

c)   The "it's up to others" syndrome

All the findings presented in this study show that even under today's conditions a substantial impact on modal choice could be achieved, simply if this were what we all wanted. But "all" means not just others, but ourselves. And "want" means giving up our own (apparent) comfort instead of finding excuses for it.

Everyone knows this in principle. The realisation that the biggest and most effective field for measures lies in that of subjective desires would, at the same time, be the admission that we could ourselves make behavioural changes without any personal disadvantages worth mentioning. In order to avoid having to make this -- for many (above all planners and policymakers) obviously painful -- admission, we have created an artificial system of requirements which others would have to fulfil before we would be willing to alter our behaviour ourselves.

This is clear, for example, in the case of the present debate over public transport: "Yes, if public transport were faster, more frequent, cheaper, more comfortable, cleaner, safer, etc., then...".

In connection with these three syndromes, non-motorised transport has a key role, for given the relatively short distances which we cover in the towns, as in the past, it is not so easy to find convincing excuses to justify our own comfort. Walking, in particular, as a possibility which in most cases requires virtually no further preconditions, would be the ideal opportunity to rediscover that mobility even without motorised help is often possible and can even be pleasurable.

We do not dispute the fact that there are at present trips for which a switch from motorised private transport to alternative modes would be difficult. But the reasons justifying these "impossible cases" must not be allowed to become excuses for the "possible cases".

FIGURES

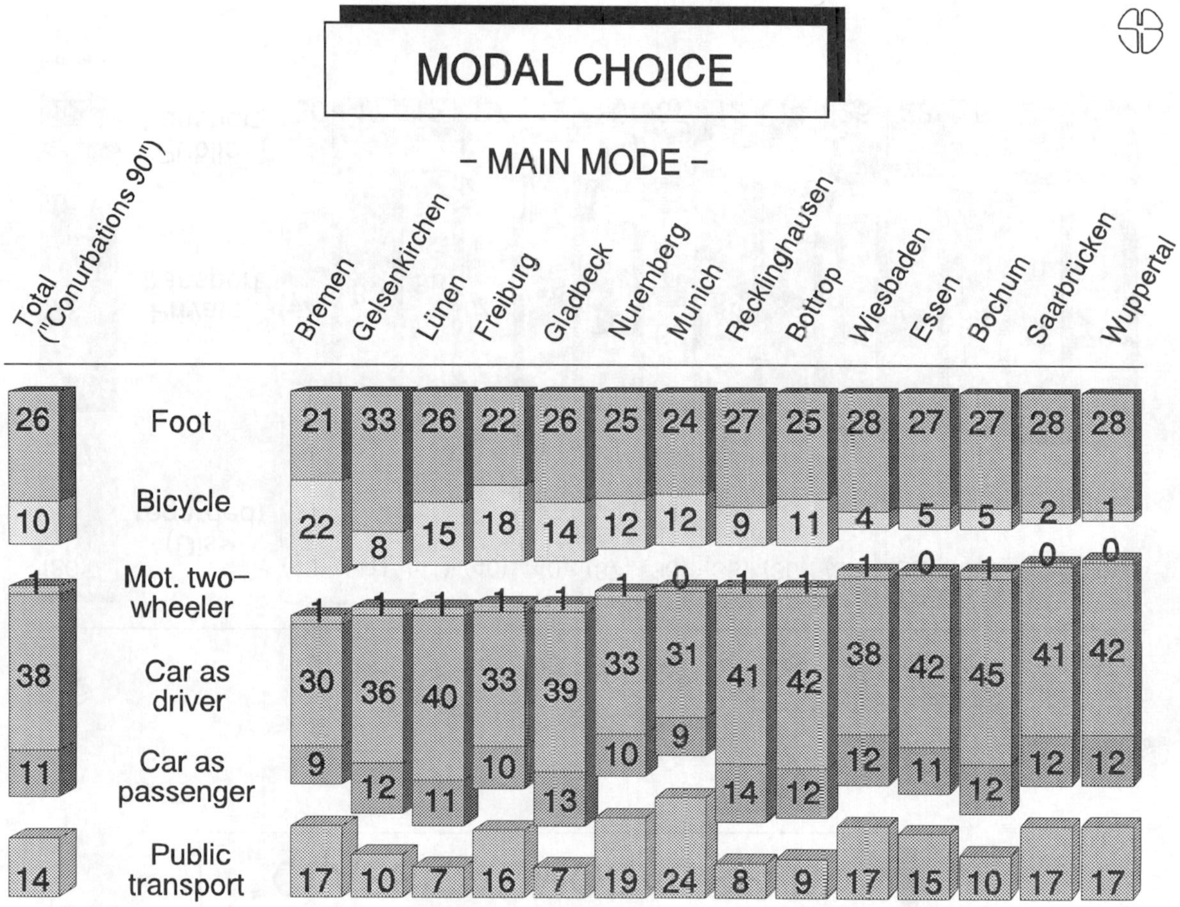

MODAL CHOICE

– MAIN MODE –

	Bremen	Gelsenkirchen	Lünen	Freiburg	Gladbeck	Nuremberg	Munich	Recklinghausen	Bottrop	Wiesbaden	Essen	Bochum	Saarbrücken	Wuppertal
Foot	21	33	26	22	26	25	24	27	25	28	27	27	28	28
Bicycle	22	8	15	18	14	12	12	9	11	4	5	5	2	1
Mot. two-wheeler	1		1	1	1	1	0	1	1	1	0	1	0	0
Car as driver	30	36	40	33	39	33	31	41	42	38	42	45	41	42
Car as passenger	9	12	11	10	13	10	9	14	12	12	11	12	12	12
Public transport	17	10	7	16	7	19	24	8	9	17	15	10	17	17

0 = less than 0,5%

Total ("Conurbations 90")

Foot	26
Bicycle	10
Mot. two-wheeler	1
Car as driver	38
Car as passenger	11
Public transport	14

Figure 1

CLASSICAL MODAL SPLIT

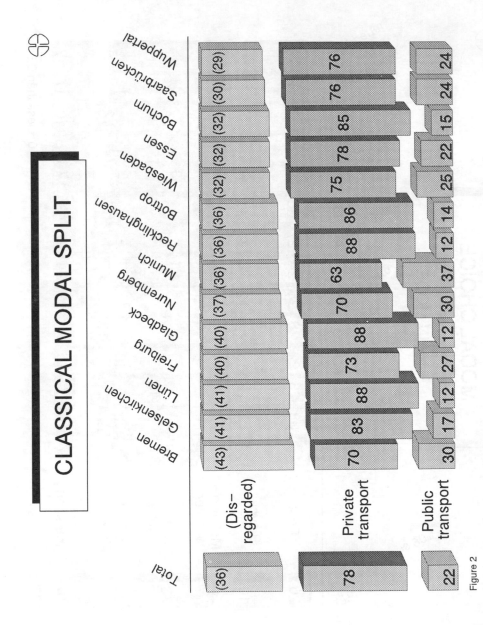

Figure 2

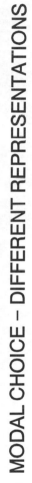

MODAL CHOICE – DIFFERENT REPRESENTATIONS
– "CONURBATIONS 90" –

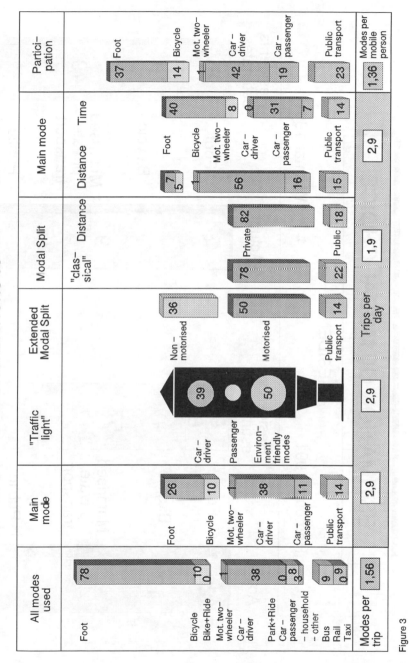

Figure 3

27

ESTIMATION OF MODAL CHOICE

– RESIDENTS –

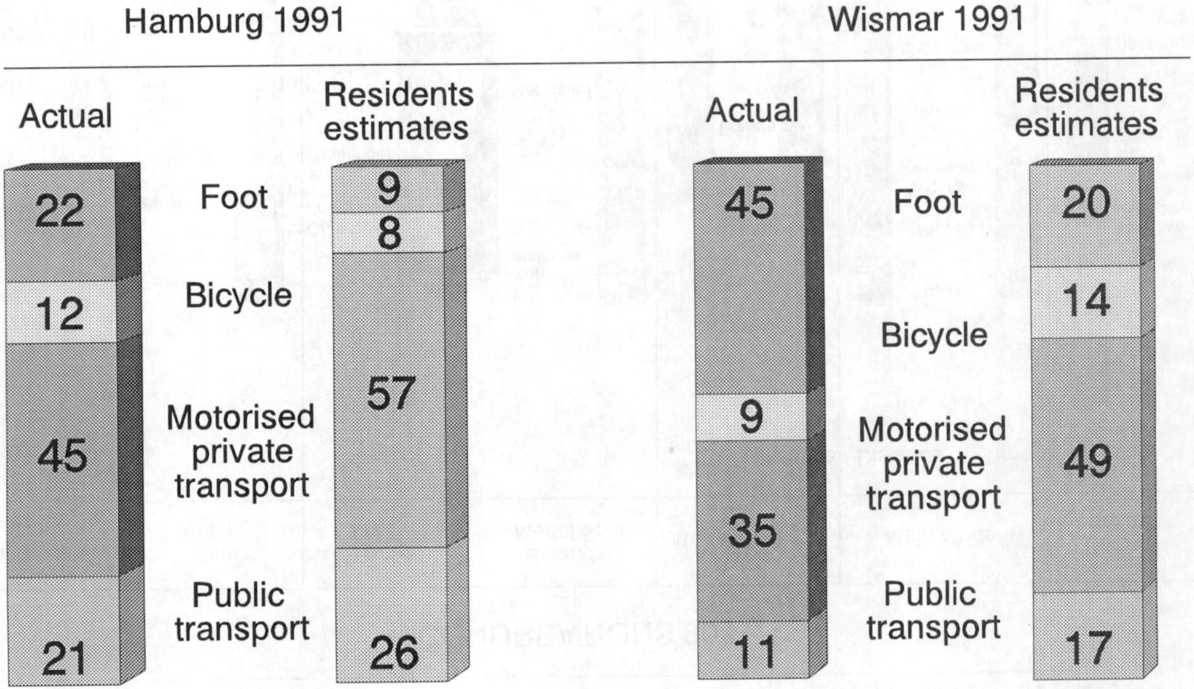

Figure 4

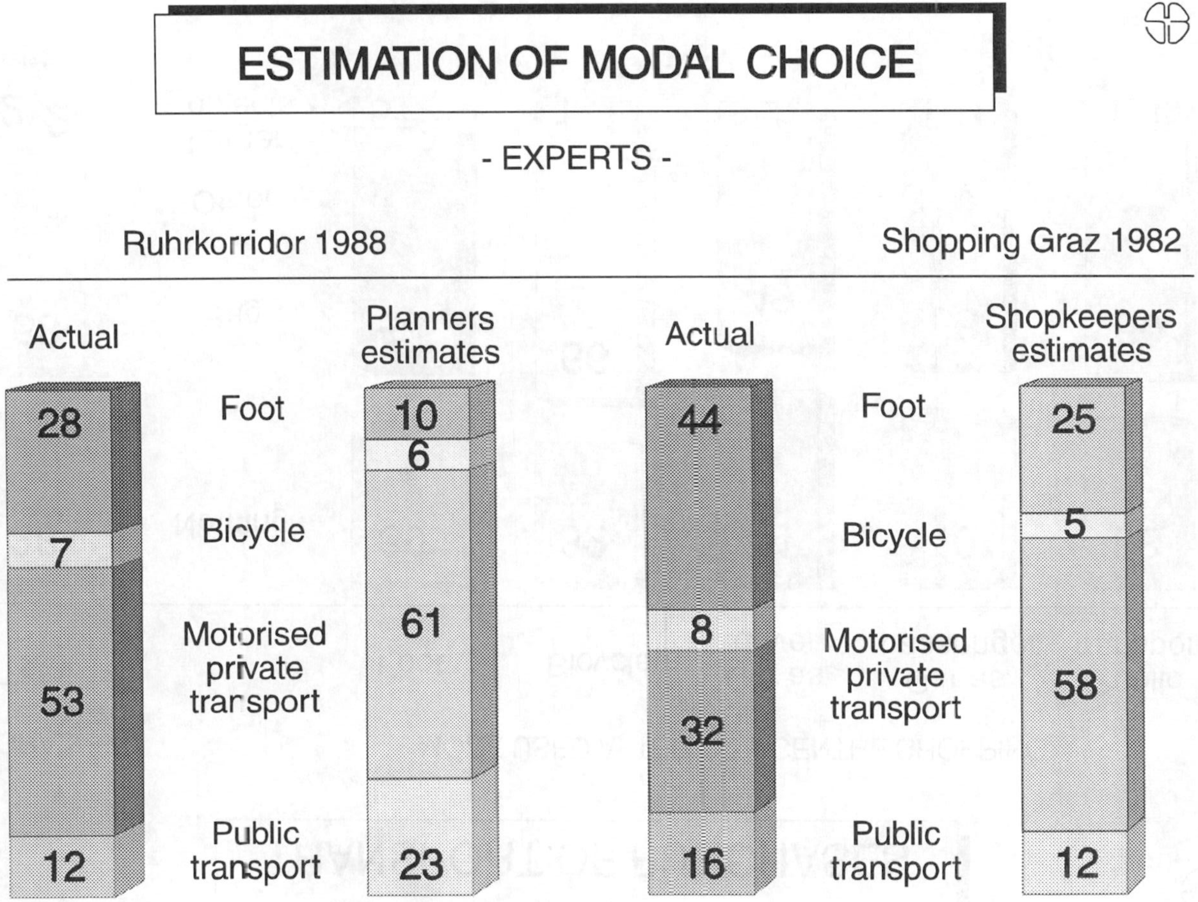

ESTIMATION OF MODAL CHOICE

- EXPERTS -

Ruhrkorridor 1988

Shopping Graz 1982

Actual

Planners estimates

Foot
28
10

Bicycle
7
6

Motorised private transport
53
61

Public transport
12
23

Actual

Shopkeepers estimates

Foot
44
25

Bicycle
8
5

Motorised private transport
32
58

Public transport
16
12

Figure 5

TRANSPORT OF PURCHASES

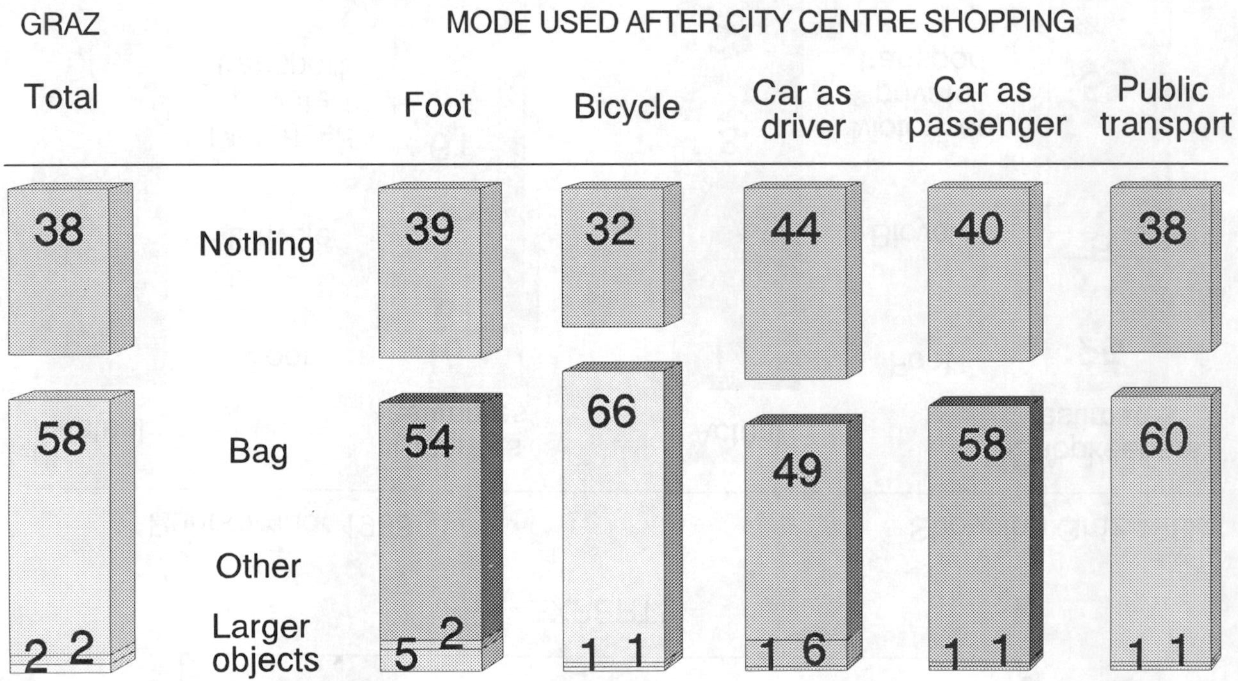

MODE USED AFTER CITY CENTRE SHOPPING

GRAZ

	Total	Foot	Bicycle	Car as driver	Car as passenger	Public transport
Nothing	38	39	32	44	40	38
Bag	58	54	66	49	58	60
Other	2	2	1	1	1	1
Larger objects	2	5	1	6	1	1

Figure 6

MODAL CHOICE – "CONURBATIONS 90" TRAFFIC LIGHT

– All trips, all days, all persons –

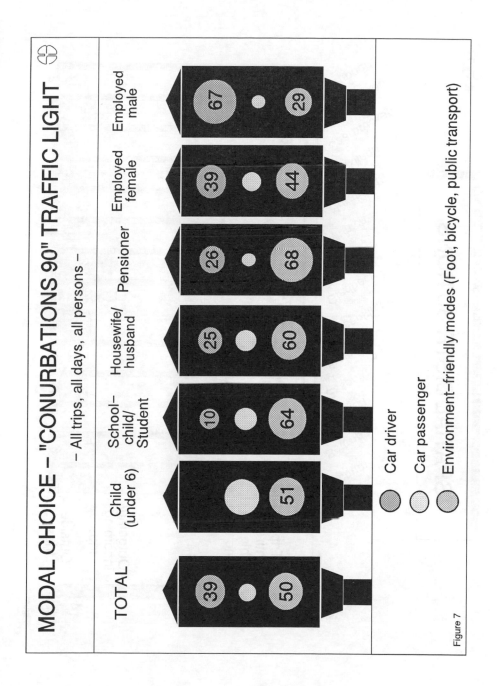

TOTAL | Child (under 6) | School-child/Student | Housewife/husband | Pensioner | Employed female | Employed male

- Car driver
- Car passenger
- Environment-friendly modes (Foot, bicycle, public transport)

Figure 7

SPATIAL DISTRIBUTIONS

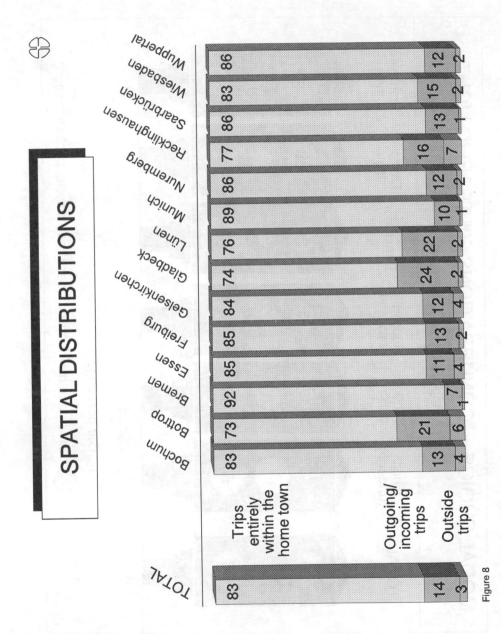

Figure 8

MODAL CHOICE

– "CONURBATIONS 90" –

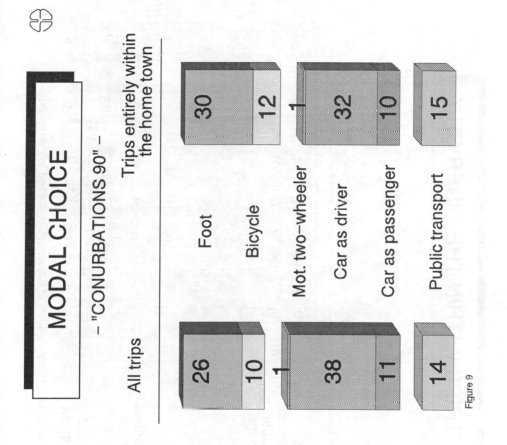

	All trips	Trips entirely within the home town
Foot	26	30
Bicycle	10	12
Mot. two–wheeler	1	1
Car as driver	38	32
Car as passenger	11	10
Public transport	14	15

Figure 9

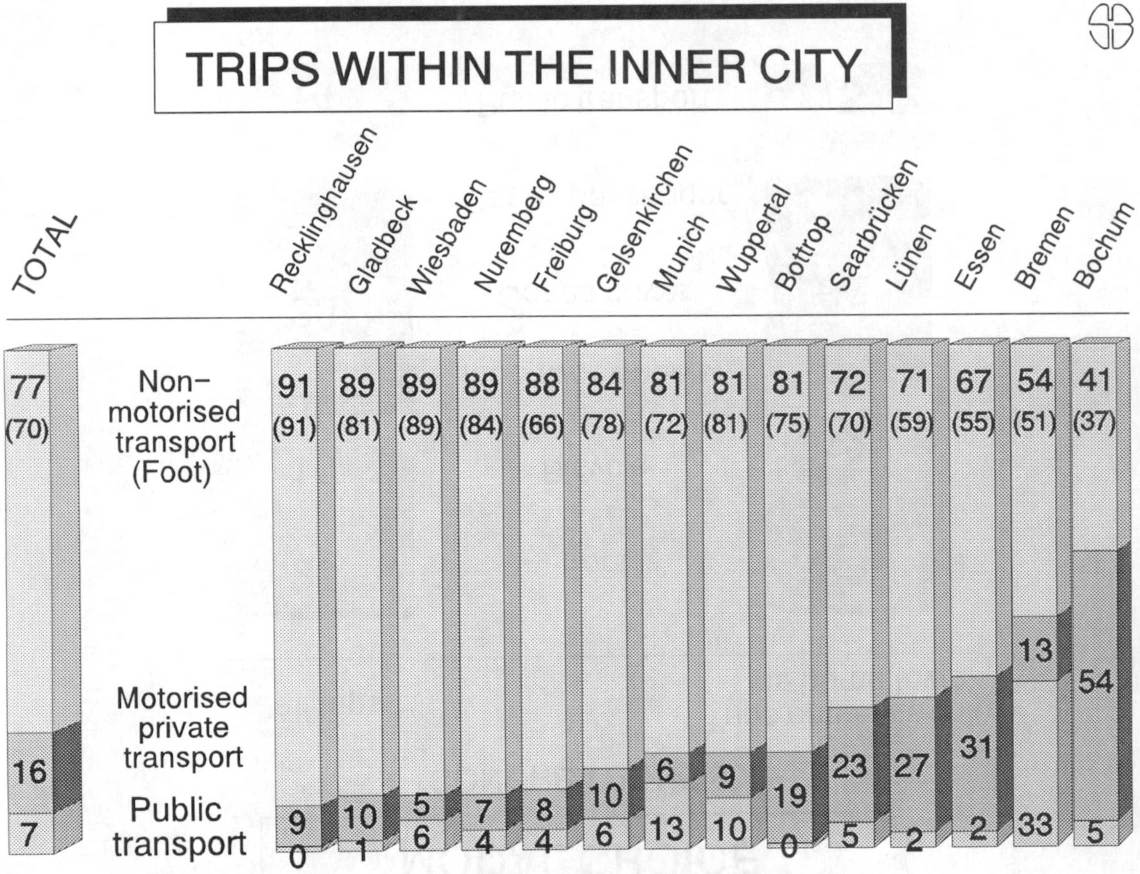

TRIPS WITHIN THE INNER CITY

	Non-motorised transport (Foot)	Motorised private transport	Public transport
Bochum	41 (37)	54	5
Bremen	54 (51)	13	33
Essen	67 (55)	31	2
Lünen	71 (59)	27	2
Saarbrücken	72 (70)	23	5
Bottrop	81 (75)	19	0
Wuppertal	81 (81)	9	10
Munich	81 (72)	6	13
Gelsenkirchen	84 (78)	10	6
Freiburg	88 (66)	8	4
Nuremberg	89 (84)	7	4
Wiesbaden	89 (89)	5	6
Gladbeck	89 (81)	10	1
Recklinghausen	91 (91)	9	0
TOTAL	77 (70)	16	7

Motorised = Private transport (car as driver or passenger, motorised two-wheeler)

Figure 10

34

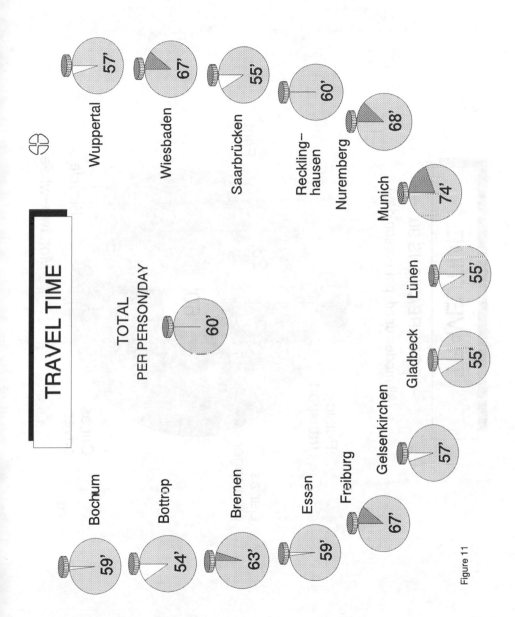

TRAVEL TIME

TOTAL PER PERSON/DAY

Wuppertal 57'
Wiesbaden 67'
Saarbrücken 55'
Recklinghausen 60'
Nuremberg 68'
Munich 74'
Lünen 55'
Gladbeck 55'
Gelsenkirchen 57'
Freiburg 67'
Essen 59'
Bremen 63'
Bottrop 54'
Bochum 59'

60'

Figure 11

35

TRAVEL TIME

– "CONURBATIONS 90" –
(All modes used, per person/day)

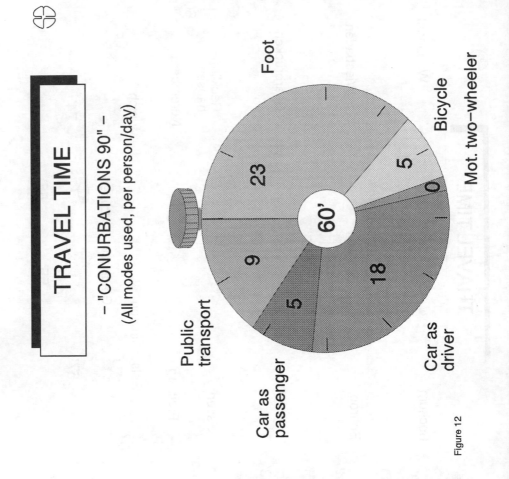

Foot

Bicycle

Mot. two-wheeler

Car as driver

Car as passenger

Public transport

23

5

0

18

5

9

60'

Figure 12

36

STAGES IN DOOR-TO-DOOR JOURNEYS

– "CONURBATIONS 90" –

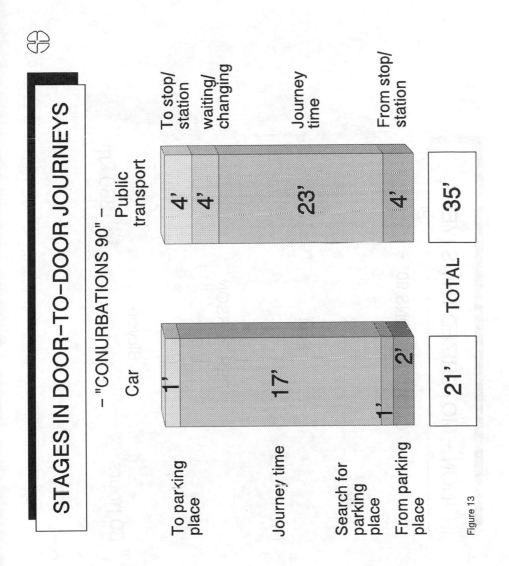

Figure 13

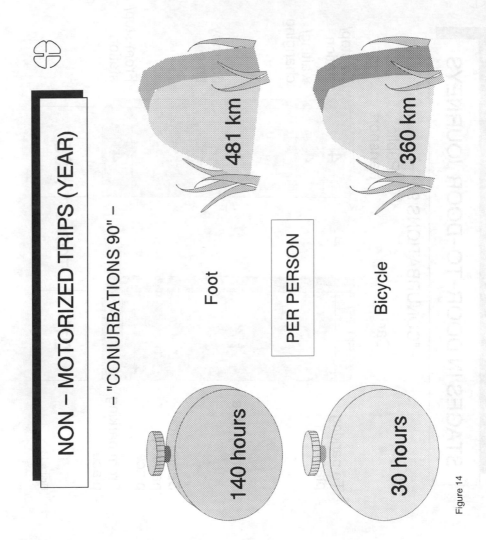

NON – MOTORIZED TRIPS (YEAR)

– "CONURBATIONS 90" –

481 km

Foot

PER PERSON

360 km

Bicycle

140 hours

30 hours

Figure 14

38

ACTIVITIES PER PERSON

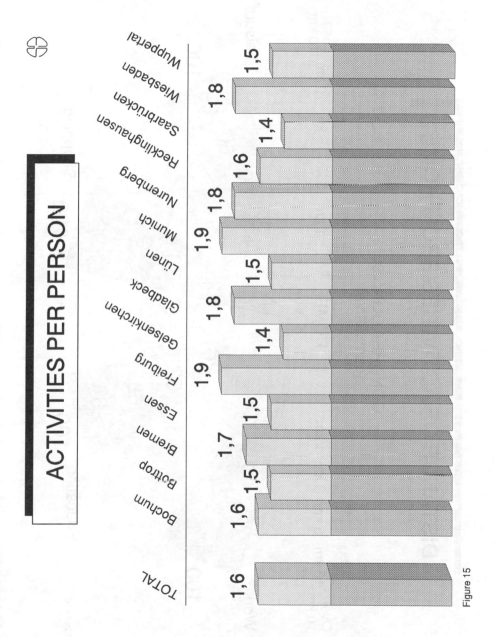

Figure 15

39

DISTANCE OF ACTIVITIES FROM HOME

– "CONURBATIONS 90" –
(cumulative)

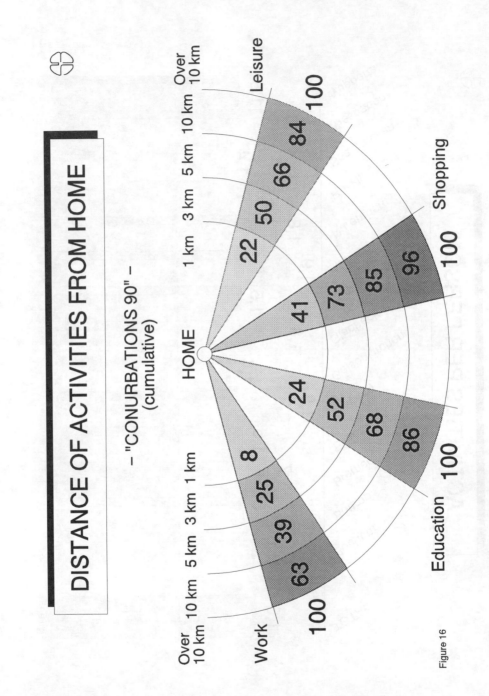

Figure 16

TRIPS PER PERSON

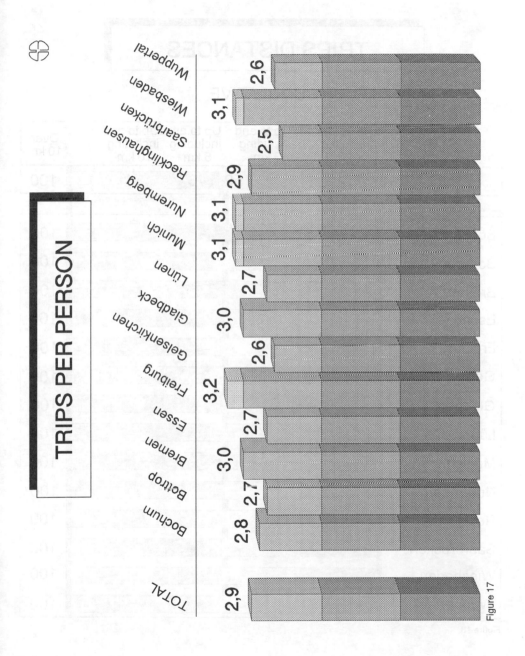

Figure 17

TOTAL	2,9
Bochum	2,8
Bottrop	2,7
Bremen	3,0
Essen	2,7
Freiburg	3,2
Gelsenkirchen	2,6
Gladbeck	3,0
Lünen	2,7
Munich	3,1
Nuremberg	3,1
Recklinghausen	2,9
Saarbrücken	2,5
Wiesbaden	3,1
Wuppertal	2,6

41

TRIPS DISTANCES

– CUMULATIVE –

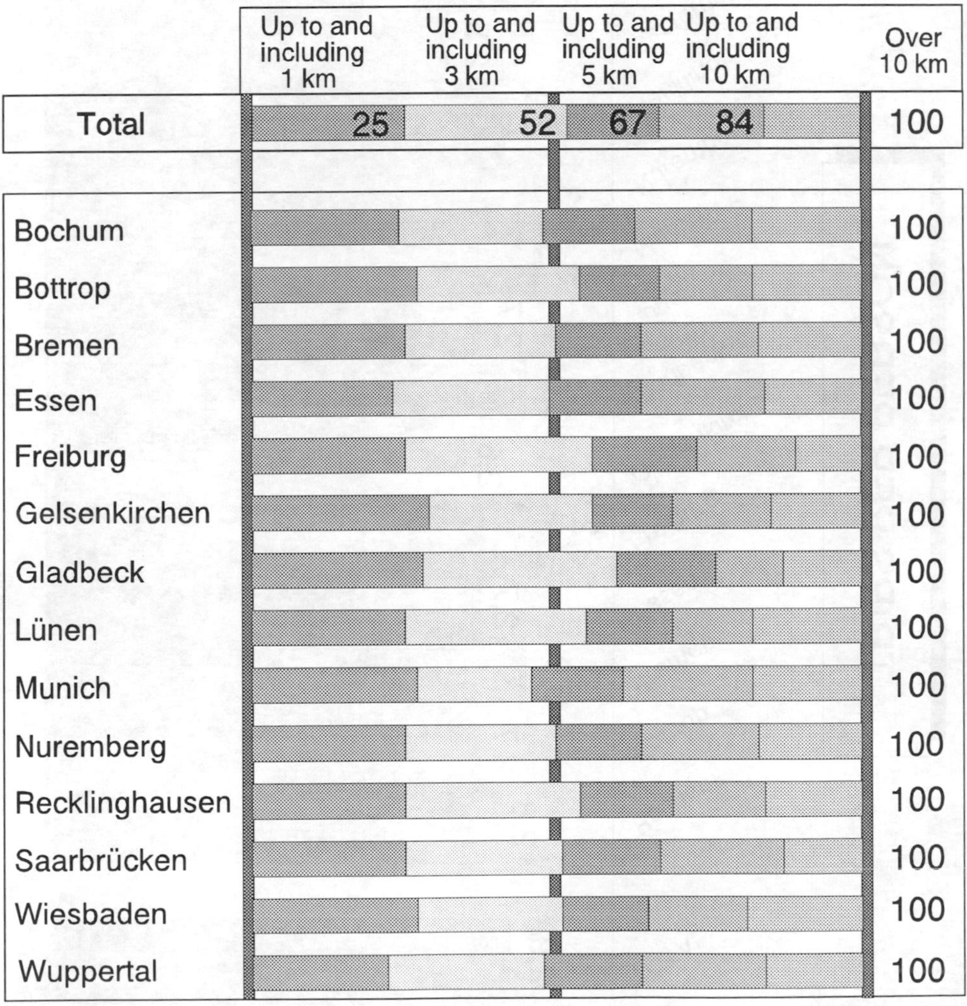

	Up to and including 1 km	Up to and including 3 km	Up to and including 5 km	Up to and including 10 km	Over 10 km
Total	25	52	67	84	100
Bochum					100
Bottrop					100
Bremen					100
Essen					100
Freiburg					100
Gelsenkirchen					100
Gladbeck					100
Lünen					100
Munich					100
Nuremberg					100
Recklinghausen					100
Saarbrücken					100
Wiesbaden					100
Wuppertal					100

Figure 18

TRIP – DISTANCES

– CUMULATIVE –

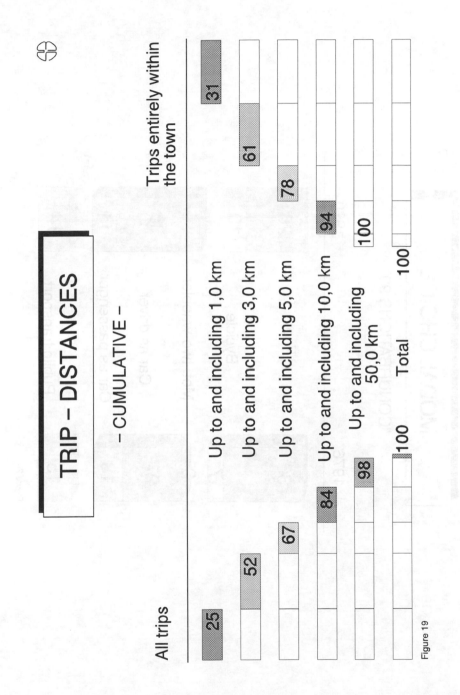

All trips

Trips entirely within the town

Up to and including 1,0 km — 25 / 31

Up to and including 3,0 km — 52 / 61

Up to and including 5,0 km — 67 / 78

Up to and including 10,0 km — 84 / 94

Up to and including 50,0 km — 98 / 100

Total — 100 / 100

Figure 19

43

MODAL CHOICE

- "CONURBATIONS 90" -

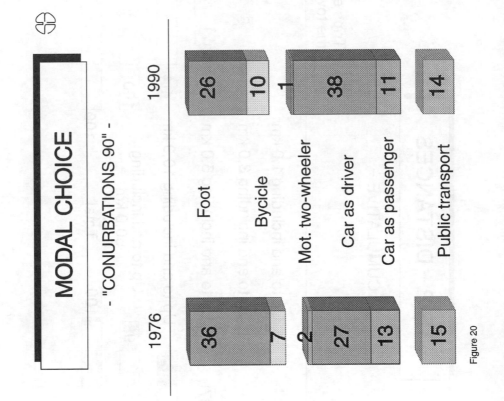

	1976	1990
Foot	36	26
Bycicle	7	10
Mot. two-wheeler	2	1
Car as driver	27	38
Car as passenger	13	11
Public transport	15	14

Figure 20

MOBILITY INDICATORS
- "CONURBATIONS 90" -

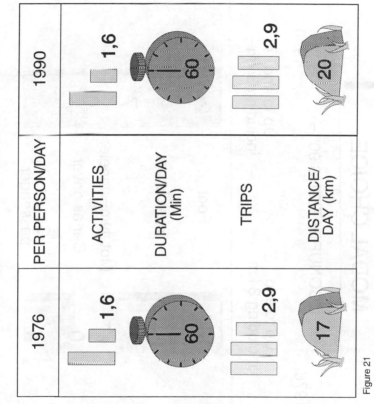

1976	PER PERSON/DAY	1990
1,6	ACTIVITIES	1,6
60	DURATION/DAY (Min)	60
2,9	TRIPS	2,9
17	DISTANCE/ DAY (km)	20

Figure 21

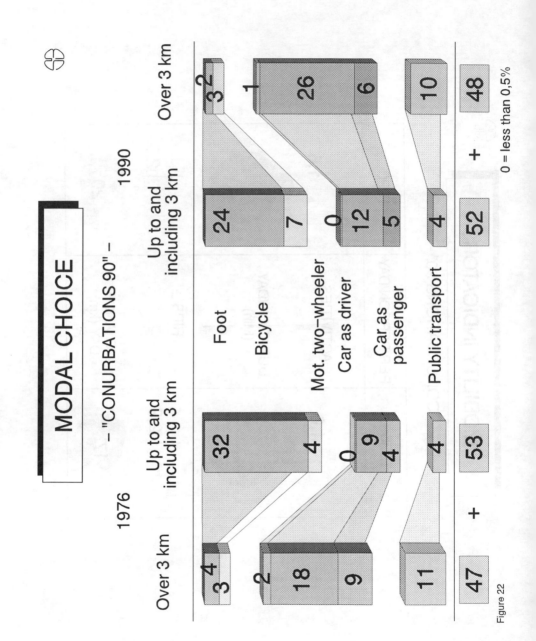

MODAL CHOICE
– "CONURBATIONS 90" –

1976   1990

Figure 22

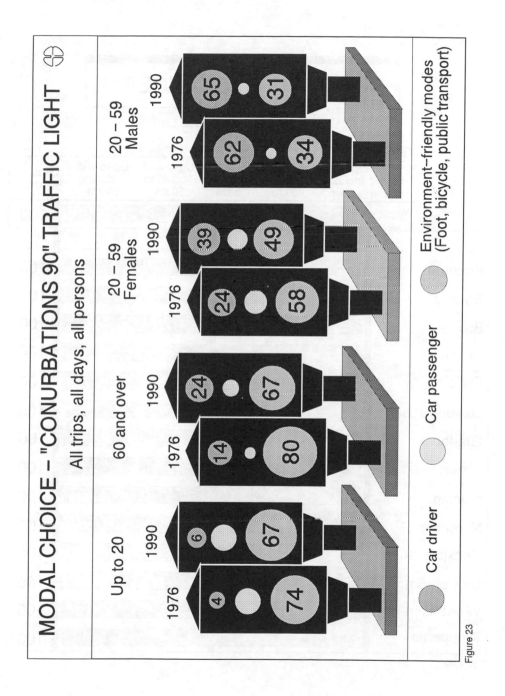

Figure 23

CAR TRIP DISTANCES

– CUMULATIVE –

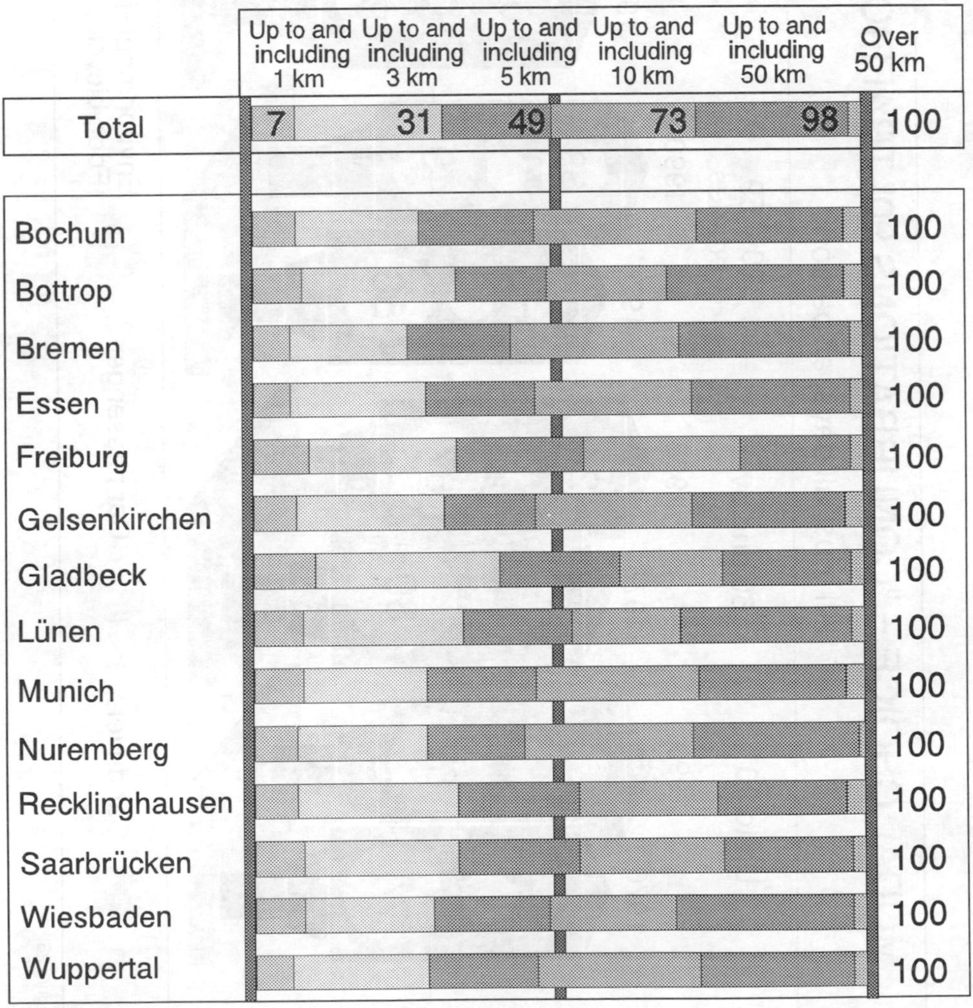

	Up to and including 1 km	Up to and including 3 km	Up to and including 5 km	Up to and including 10 km	Up to and including 50 km	Over 50 km
Total	7	31	49	73	98	100
Bochum						100
Bottrop						100
Bremen						100
Essen						100
Freiburg						100
Gelsenkirchen						100
Gladbeck						100
Lünen						100
Munich						100
Nuremberg						100
Recklinghausen						100
Saarbrücken						100
Wiesbaden						100
Wuppertal						100

Figure 24

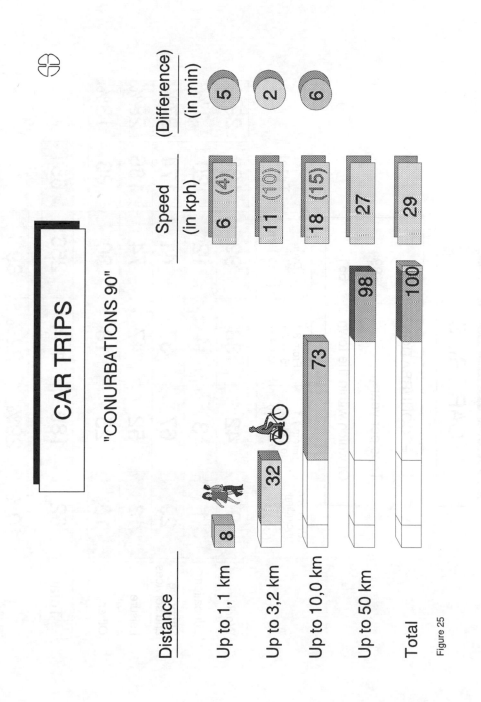

CAR TRIPS

"CONURBATIONS 90"

Distance		Speed (in kph)	(Difference) (in min)
Up to 1,1 km	8	6 (4)	5
Up to 3,2 km	32	11 (10)	2
Up to 10,0 km	73	18 (15)	6
Up to 50 km	98	27	
Total	100	29	

Figure 25

49

CAR TRIPS

– "CONURBATIONS 90" –

Trips per year: 889

Of which within the town: 651

	Up to and including 1,0 km (⌀0,8 km)	From 1,1 to 3 km (⌀2,4 km)	From 3,1 to 5 km (⌀4,4 km)	Over 5 km (⌀10,1 km)	Total	
Work	9	42	38	99	188	29%
Education	1	3	4	12	20	3%
Shopping and services	29	67	37	41	174	27%
Leisure	13	52	47	74	186	28%
Other	10	25	18	30	83	13%
Total	62	189	144	256	651	
	10%	29%	22%	39%		

Figure 26

50

CAR TRIPS (YEAR)

– "CONURBATIONS 90" –

Trips within
the conurbation

Possibility for reduction

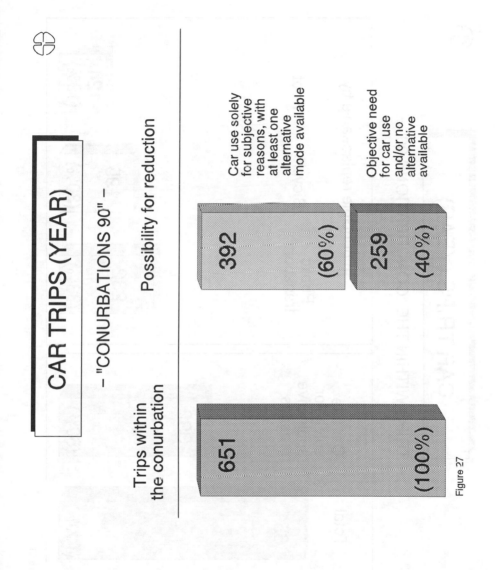

651
(100%)

392
(60%)

Car use solely
for subjective
reasons, with
at least one
alternative
mode available

259
(40%)

Objective need
for car use
and/or no
alternative
available

Figure 27

CAR TRIPS (YEAR)

– TRIPS WITHIN THE "CONURBATIONS 90" –

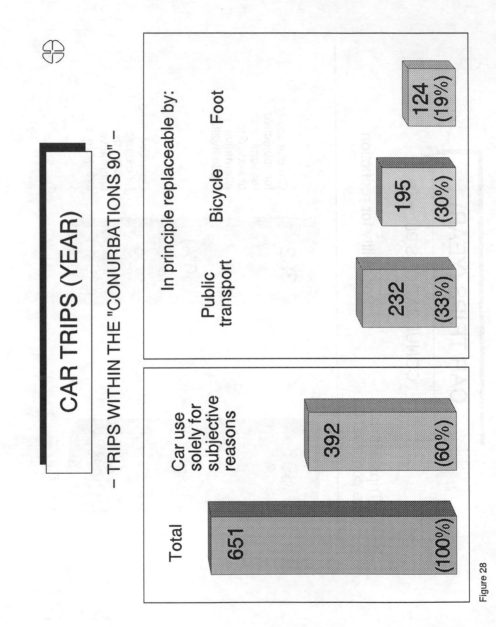

Figure 28

52

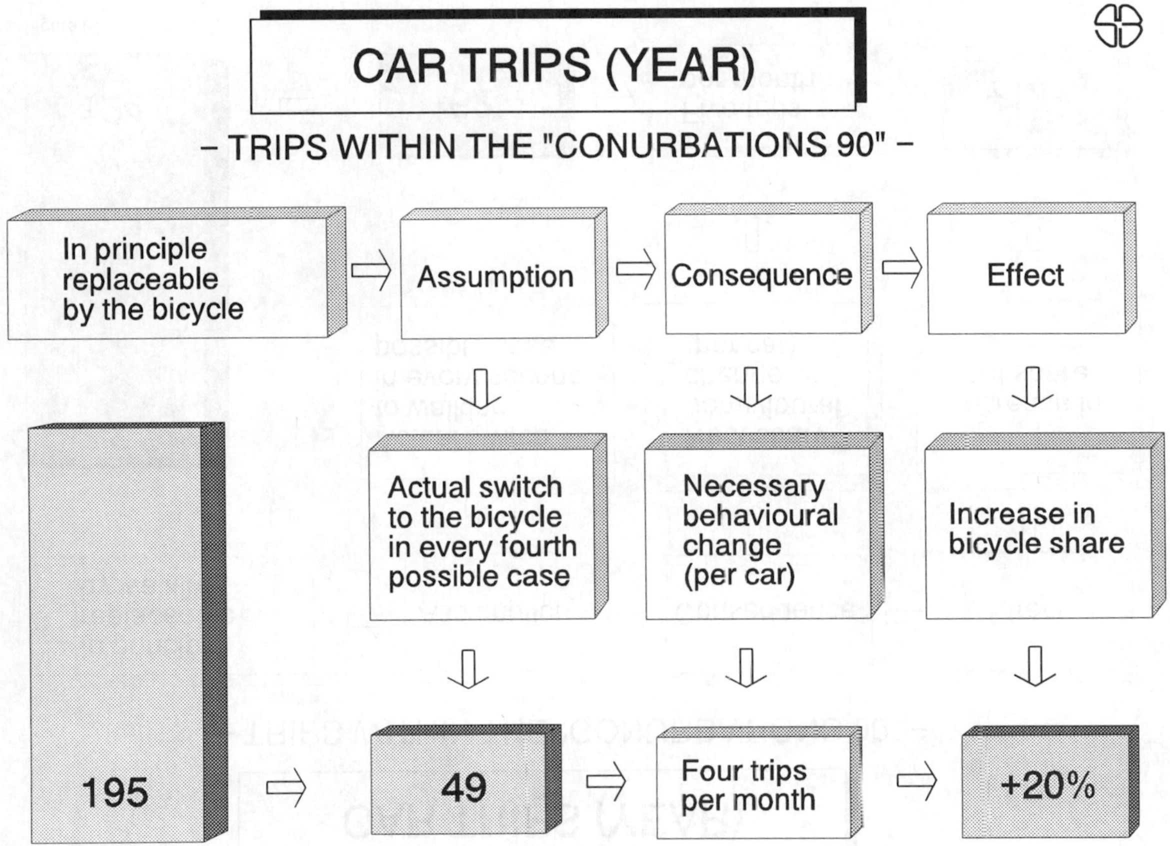

CAR TRIPS (YEAR)

– TRIPS WITHIN THE "CONURBATIONS 90" –

In principle replaceable by the bicycle	⇨	Assumption	⇨	Consequence	⇨	Effect
		Actual switch to the bicycle in every fourth possible case	⇨	Necessary behavioural change (per car)	⇨	Increase in bicycle share
195	⇨	49	⇨	Four trips per month	⇨	+20%

Figure 29

53

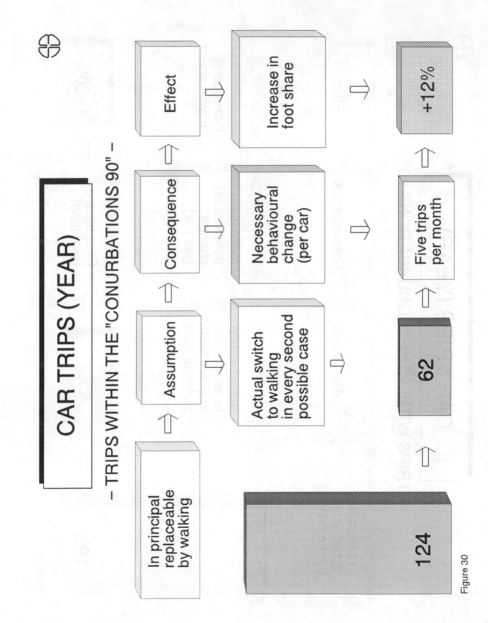

CAR TRIPS (YEAR)
– TRIPS WITHIN THE "CONURBATIONS 90" –

| In principal replaceable by walking | ⇨ | Assumption | ⇨ | Consequence | ⇨ | Effect |

124

| Actual switch to walking in every second possible case | ⇨ | Necessary behavioural change (per car) | ⇨ | Increase in foot share |

62 ⇨ Five trips per month ⇨ **+12%**

Figure 30

54

CAR TRIPS (YEAR)

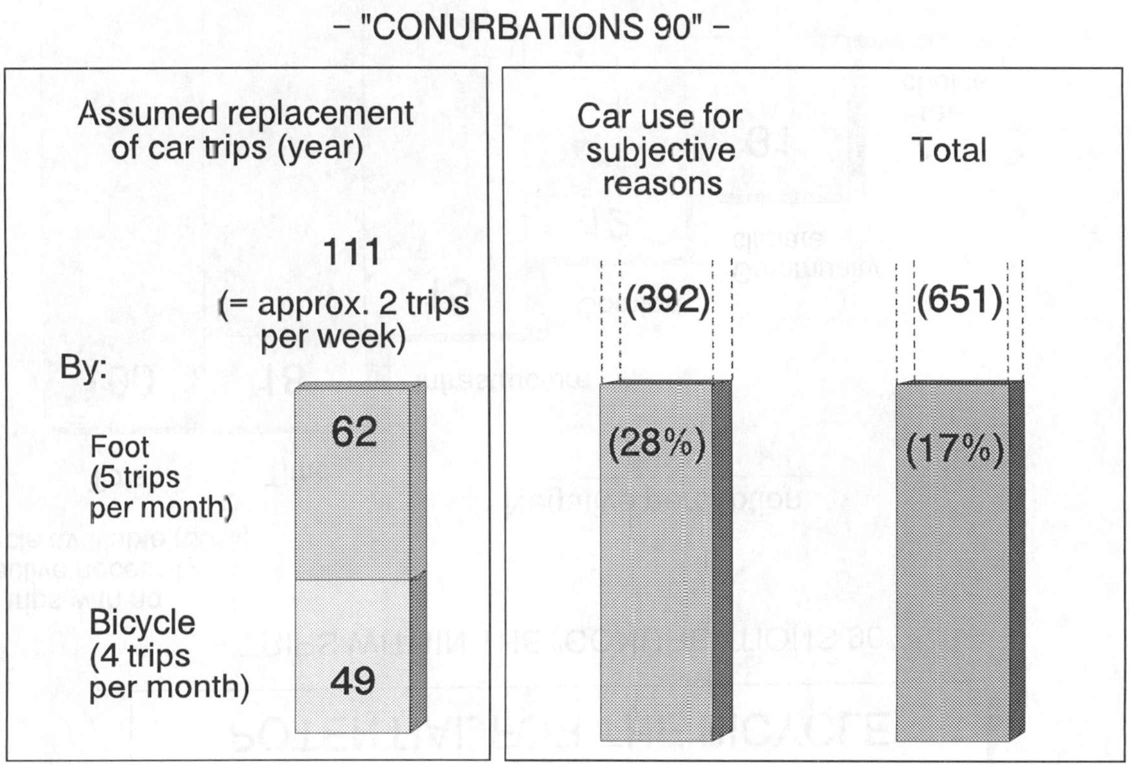

– "CONURBATIONS 90" –

Car use for
subjective
reasons

Total

(392)

(651)

(28%)

(17%)

Assumed replacement
of car trips (year)

111

(= approx. 2 trips
per week)

By:

Foot
(5 trips
per month)

62

Bicycle
(4 trips
per month)

49

Figure 31

POTENTIAL FOR THE BICYCLE

– TRIPS WITHIN THE "CONURBATIONS 90" –

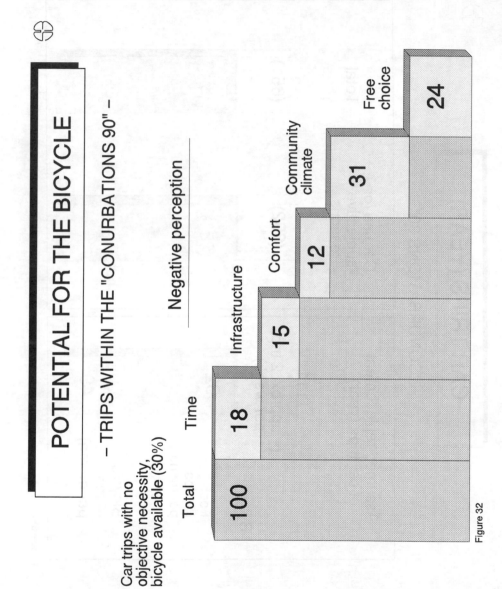

Car trips with no objective necessity, bicycle available (30%)

Negative perception

Total 100

Time 18

Infrastructure 15

Comfort 12

Community climate 31

Free choice 24

Figure 32

POTENTIAL FOR TRIPS ON FOOT

– TRIPS WITHIN THE "CONURBATIONS 90" –

Car trips with no
objective necessity,
walking possible (19%)

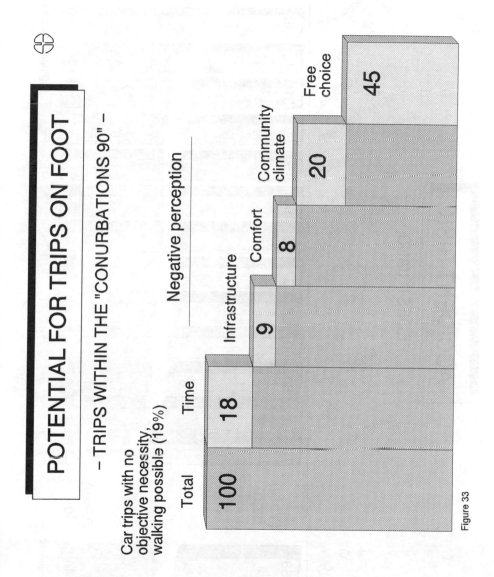

Figure 33

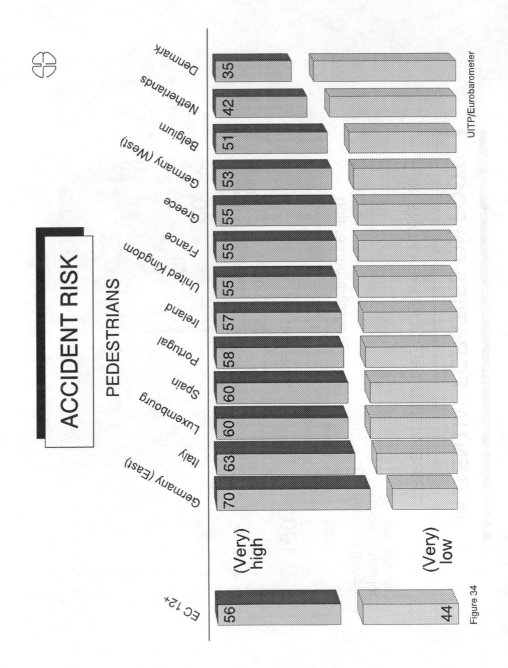

ACCIDENT RISK

PEDESTRIANS

Denmark 35
Netherlands 42
Belgium 51
Germany (West) 53
Greece 55
France 55
United Kingdom 55
Ireland 57
Portugal 58
Spain 60
Luxembourg 60
Italy 63
Germany (East) 70

(Very) high

(Very) low

EC 12+ 56 / 44

UITP/Eurobarometer

Figure 34

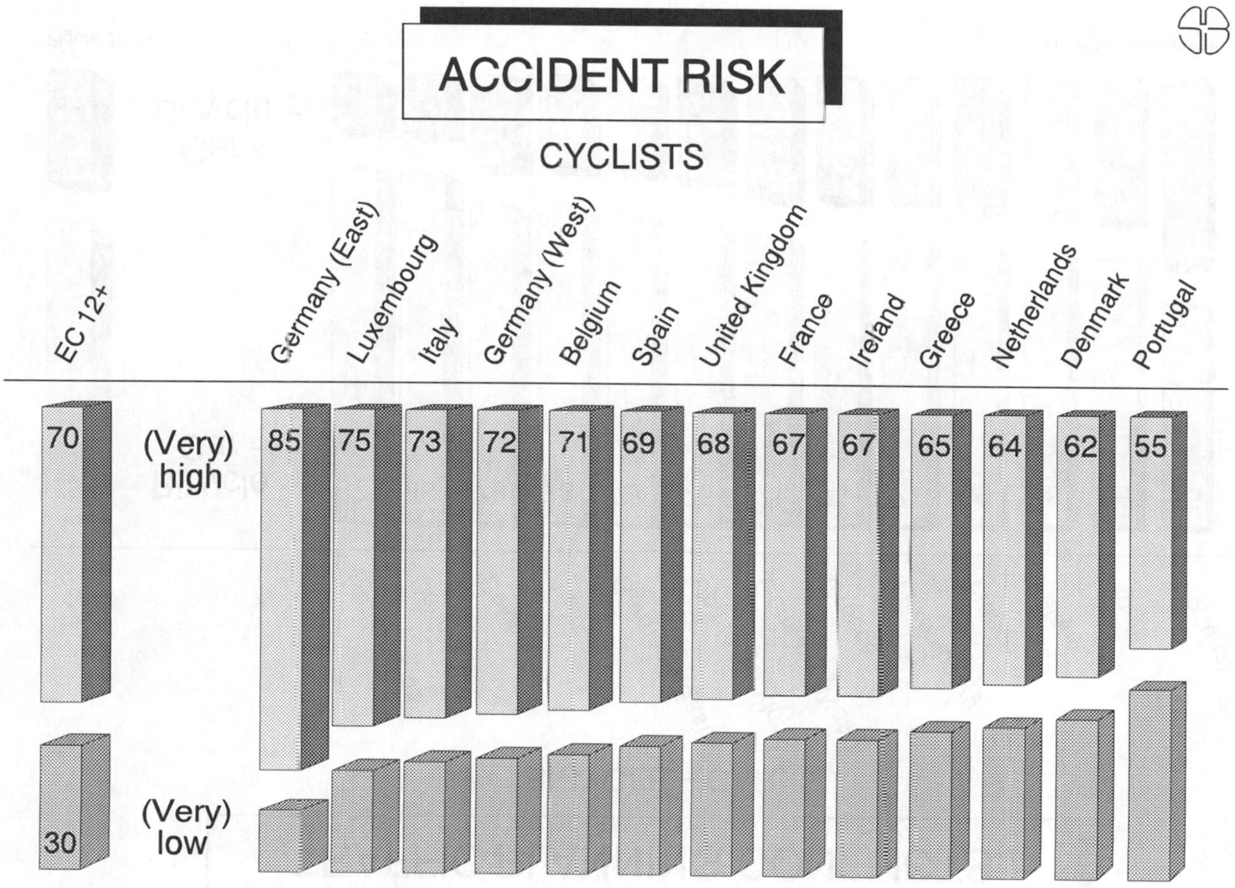

ACCIDENT RISK

CYCLISTS

Figure 35

UITP/Eurobarometer

Portugal 55
Denmark 62
Netherlands 64
Greece 65
Ireland 67
France 67
United Kingdom 68
Spain 69
Belgium 71
Germany (West) 72
Italy 73
Luxembourg 75
Germany (East) 85

(Very) high

(Very) low

EC 12+ 70 / 30

59

TRAFFIC PLANNING CONFLICTS

BICYCLE – CAR

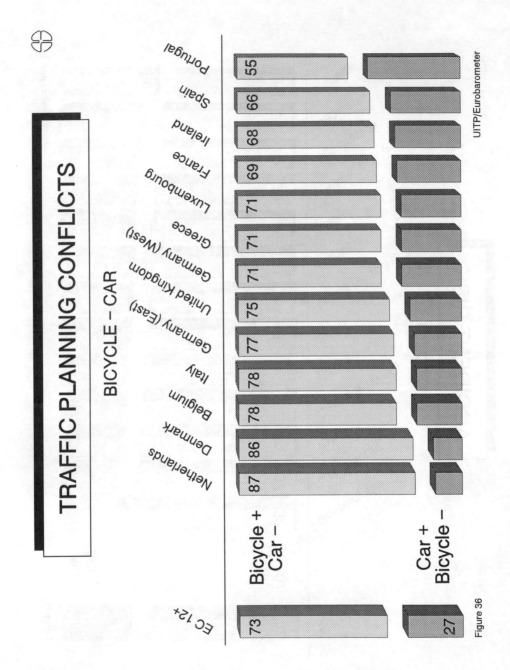

Bicycle + Car –

Country	Value
Netherlands	87
Denmark	86
Belgium	78
Italy	78
Germany (East)	77
United Kingdom	75
Germany (West)	71
Greece	71
Luxembourg	71
France	69
Ireland	68
Spain	66
Portugal	55

Car + Bicycle –

EC 12+: Bicycle + Car – 73, Car + Bicycle – 27

UITP/Eurobarometer

Figure 36

60

TRAFFIC PLANNING CONFLICTS

FOOT – CAR

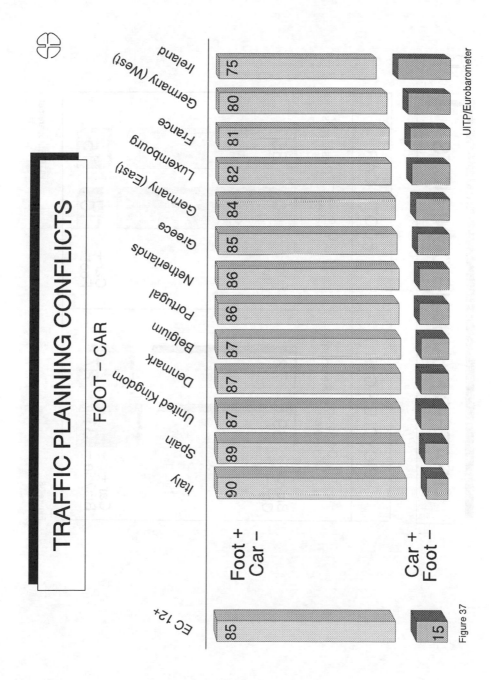

Foot +
Car –

Ireland	75
Germany (West)	80
France	81
Luxembourg	82
Germany (East)	84
Greece	85
Netherlands	86
Portugal	86
Belgium	87
Denmark	87
United Kingdom	87
Spain	89
Italy	90

Car +
Foot –

EC 12+ : 85 / 15

UITP/Eurobarometer

Figure 37

TRAFFIC PLANNING CONFLICTS

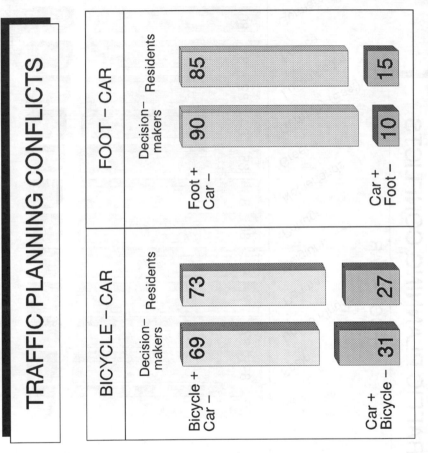

BICYCLE – CAR

FOOT – CAR

Decision–makers   Residents

Bicycle + Car –   69   73

Car + Bicycle –   31   27

Decision–makers   Residents

Foot + Car –   90   85

Car + Foot –   10   15

UITP/Eurobarometer

Figure 38

62

TRAFFIC PLANNING CONFLICTS

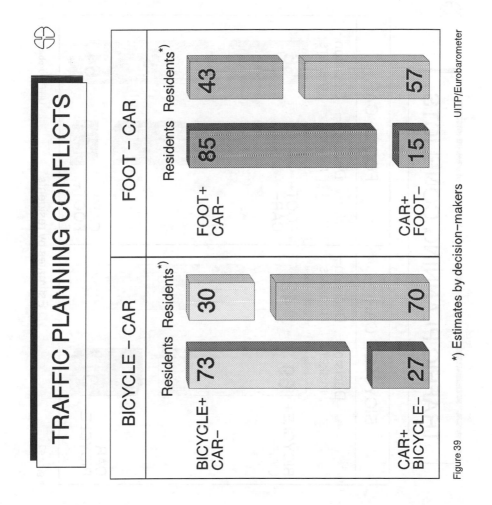

Figure 39

*) Estimates by decision-makers

UITP/Eurobarometer

TRAFFIC PLANNING CONFLICTS

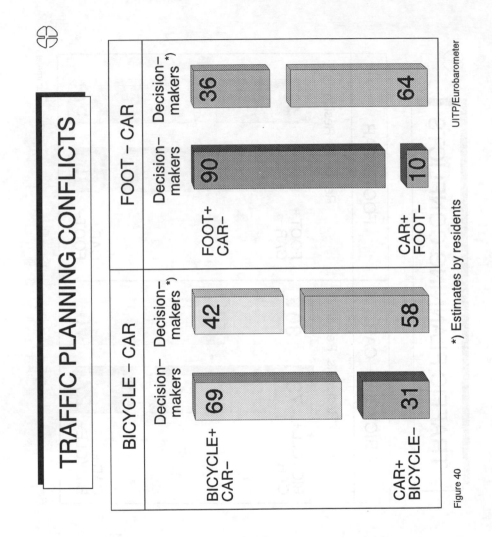

BICYCLE – CAR

Decision–makers | Decision–makers *)
BICYCLE+ CAR– : 69 | 42
CAR+ BICYCLE– : 31 | 58

FOOT – CAR

Decision–makers | Decision–makers *)
FOOT+ CAR– : 90 | 36
CAR+ FOOT– : 10 | 64

UITP/Eurobarometer

*) Estimates by residents

Figure 40

64

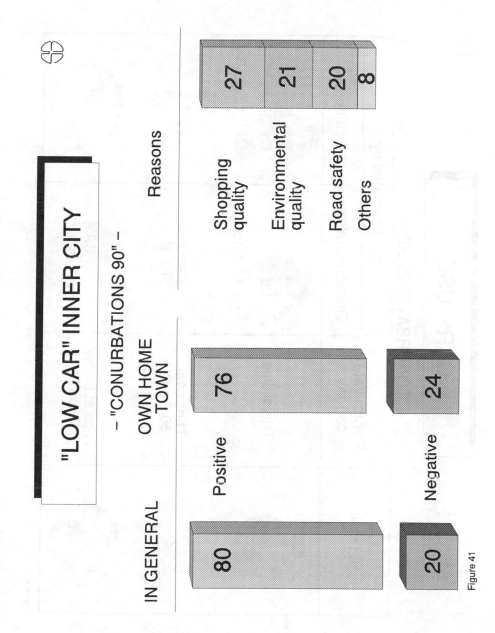

Figure 41

65

CAR – USE

– "CONURBATIONS 90" –

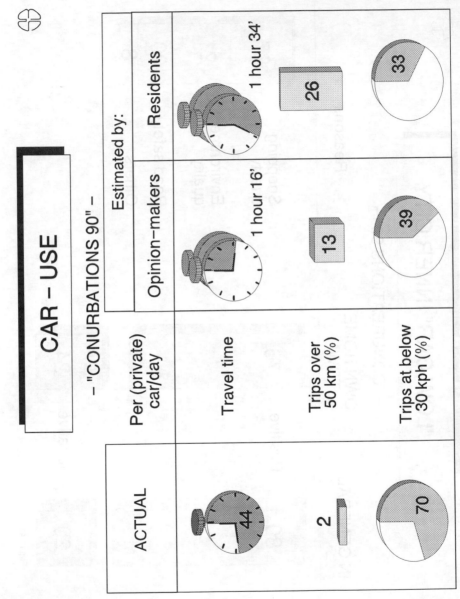

Per (private) car/day	Estimated by:	
	Opinion-makers	Residents
Travel time	1 hour 16'	1 hour 34'
Trips over 50 km (%)	13	26
Trips at below 30 kph (%)	39	33

ACTUAL
44
2
70

Figure 42

BIBLIOGRAPHY

Bremer Strassenbahn AG: Mobilität in Bremen, 1991.

Ministerium für Stadtentwicklung und Verkehr des Landes Nordrhein-Westfalen, Düsseldorf: Trendwende zum ÖPNV, 1992.

Stadt Lünen: Mobilität in Lünen, im Rahmen des Modellvorhabens "Fahrradfreundliches Lünen", 1989.

Verkchrsgemeinschaft Freiburg: Mobilität in Freiburg, 1989.

Stadt Gladbeck: Mobilität in Gladbeck, im Rahmen des Modellvorhabens "Fahrradfreundliches Gladbeck", 1989.

VAG Verkehrs-Aktiengesellschaft Nürnberg: Mobilität in Nürnberg, 1989.

Umweltschutzreferat München: Mobilität in München, 1989.

Stadtwerke Wiesbaden AG (ESWE): Mobilität in Wiesbaden, 1990.

Gesellschaft für Strassenbahnen im Saarland, AG: Mobilität in Saarbrücken, 1989.

Wuppertaler Stadtwerke AG: Mobilität in Wuppertal, 1991.

European Conference of Ministers of Transport: Psychological Determinants of User Behaviour, Round Table 34, Paris, 1977.

Umweltbundesamt: Modellvorhaben "Fahrradfreudliche Stadt", Berlin, 1988.

SOCIALDATA: Kleine Fibel vom Zufussgehen und anderen Merkwürdigkeiten, München, 1992.

UITP: Einschätzungen zur Mobilität in Europa, Brüssel/München, 1992.

FRANCE

A. BIEBER

Directeur pour la Prospective des Transports
INRETS
Arcueil
France

MECHANISED SHORT-DISTANCE PASSENGER TRANSPORT ELEMENTS FOR A DISCUSSION

SUMMARY

Arcueil, December 1992

SUMMARY

1. INTRODUCTION

In this paper we attempt a brief synthesis of the many but disparate works produced over the past hundred years or so on the development of transport modes **specially adapted** to the needs of people wishing to cover **short distances** by means other than the traditional modes (foot, cycle and car)[1].

We stress "specially adapted" in order to define the field covered. The fact is that in accordance with the old dictum that *What can do more can do less*, we should recall that the conventional public transport modes can, with certain modifications, be operated over distances shorter than those at which they run at the "optimum". To give an example, the metro and bus in intra-mural Paris serve rather well for short-distance movements: say, those a little too long to be covered comfortably on foot, or roughly between 400 and 2 000 metres. But we are well aware, in choosing this example, that the service quality is due to a characteristic which has become rare in the world of public transport, i.e. a very dense and regular mesh of lines.

When the necessary historical conditions (compact town, very voluntarist public transport policy) are not present, it often happens that the question arises of transporting people over limited distances by some *ad hoc* mode. We would say that historically these *ad hoc* modes have appeared over the past hundred years or so in three types of case, only one of which really concerns us here:

1. Short **vertical** distances are perfectly well catered for by lifts and escalators. In this case, gravity makes "on foot" solutions very unpleasant beyond a difference in level of about 10 or 15 metres. Since the mid-nineteenth century, with ever higher buildings, there has thus been an undeniable need here for mechanical transport, which has given rise to a very buoyant industry (which has no particular problems and to which we shall not refer again);

2. Short **oblique** distances, historically served by funiculars and, more rarely, cable cars. Here, after a boom period at the end of the

nineteenth century, the urban market has tended to decline with the spread of the motor car and bus, which has made it possible for the road modes to handle traffic between the higher and lower parts of many historic urban sites (cf. Lisbon, Valparaiso, Algiers, Lyons, Laon, to cite just a few examples).

3. Short and medium distances "**on the level**", for which the spur of need is absent, at least at first sight:

    -- Firstly, because walking (or cycling) is not made difficult by slopes;
    -- Secondly, because the conventional modes are there to (also) cover these short distances, close to those which can be covered "comfortably" on foot;
    -- Lastly, because -- and this seems to us very important -- the absence of any great discomfort made it impossible to introduce one of the two economic practices inseparable, in the late nineteenth century, for the development of public transport networks: either "internalisation" pure and simple of the costs in those of a larger economic unit (the building in the case of lifts and escalators) or very large subsidies (traditional in the case of normal urban public transport).

This absence of the spur of need has not prevented inventors from being extremely prolific, but with limited results as we shall see. An initial attempt to develop a theory, made by G. Bouladon, points out the interstitial and fragile nature of the "market". The first part of the text discusses these factors.

In the second part we discuss certain aspects of the "network morphology" which is useful for the presentation of the technological families. We summarily describe the state of the art for each of these families.

In a third part we deal with the problem of outlets (or markets) and outline some questions concerning industrial prospects in order to give some (necessarily limited) idea of the future status of this activity.

2. THE NATURE OF THE PROBLEM

2.1. Historical background[2]

In the acceleration of technical progress in transport techniques which, with the coming of the electric motor, marked the second half of the nineteenth century, we must note the essential role played in the beginning by the big international exhibitions. The first known short-distance transport system was in service at the Chicago Exhibition in 1893. Over a length of 1 300 metres, a system consisting of two contiguous conveyor belts with lateral entry carried people at 5 and 10 km/h. The faster conveyor was fitted with transversal benches.

The idea and the system were taken up again at the Paris Universal Exhibition in 1900, with a few modifications (suppression of the benches and narrowing of the outside conveyors, speeds of 4 and 8 km/h). This time the loop was 3 400 metres long. History tells us that the high-speed conveyor carried almost seven million passengers in eight months. None of the 43 injury accidents recorded was serious.

Research was resumed after the First World War in France, the United Kingdom and the United States. In France, a competition was organised in 1920 under the sponsorship of the *Conseil de Paris*. The winning project (Bouchet system) was a high-speed conveyor. It was experimented with for a long time, but finally seems to have foundered in a sea of red tape. In the United Kingdom, Adkins and Lewis, who had been working on their project since 1905, installed the "Never-Stop Railway" on the site of the Imperial Exhibition at Wembley in 1924. This time the system, over a loop of 2 200 metres, comprised 88 cars, each carrying 30 passengers. They were accelerated from 2 to 16 km/h by means of a variable pitch Archimedes screw drive arrangement. The system gave entire satisfaction at the exhibition over a period of two years and was then offered to London Transport, with no success, over a period of thirty years, according to B. Richards[3].

Research was also carried out in the United States during the 1920s, but the project (M. Putnam, Continuous Transit Corporation) -- which already involved a linear motor and was intended to carry 32 000 people an hour in each direction over the famous New York route, along 42nd Street between Times Square and Grand Central, replacing the subway shuttle so well-known to New Yorkers -- never got beyond the full-scale model stage.

After the economic crisis of the 30s and the Second World War, it was in 1953 that Goodyear revived the idea of an accelerated car system for urban use. This was the Carveyor, proposed for the same major New York axis as its predecessor, and it suffered the same fate, despite the improved technology.

It was not until the 60s that a fourth inventive power appeared, Switzerland, which in its turn installed short-distance transport systems at two big international exhibitions. The "Télécanapé" and the "Habegger Minirail" were used at the Lausanne Universal Exhibition in 1964, and the second was used again at the Montreal Exhibition in 1967, where it carried 17 million people on small automatic trains running at low speed on an ultra-light overhead railway. This Habegger mini-metro was to serve two years later as example and inspiration for the *Établissement Public de Lille-Est* in drafting the calls for designs which led to the VAL.

This was in the period between 1965 and 1975 which saw the "explosion" of technological invention in the field of urban transport.

As P. Patin[4] reminds us, this was when a "systems" approach to innovations appeared, which was to lead to radical changes in the design of urban transport, with automatic operation:

-- The concept of "feeder" vehicles coming to couple to a train running at constant speed;
-- Semi-continuous car transport with stations;
-- High-speed conveyors;

and in the field of components:

-- Variable speed drive systems (deformable meshes, etc.);
-- Various anti-collision systems;
-- Point switching for rubber-tired systems;
-- Linear motors;
-- Magnetic levitation and air cushions.

The lists in Annex briefly recall the nature and history of the main methods used in the already lengthy history of short-distance transport.

As from this period of intense methodological effort, it can be seen that things evolved more rapidly "on the ground".

The first market to appear was that of the major airports, above all in the United States. Ever-bigger airports meant that mobility within them involved distances too long to be covered comfortably on foot. Complex configurations with multiple satellites (and parking areas on the land side) began to appear. The need for transport was now evident, and first AEG-Westinghouse and then other manufacturers met this need with automatic systems still close to traditional urban systems.

For their part, the big theme parks and international exhibitions constituted a second market of some importance. A third market "on the architectural scale"[5] was also now gradually emerging. Certain hotels, casinos, specialised public institutions (hospitals, universities, etc.) began to install "people-movers" which were purely internal, but nevertheless more ambitious than the traditional lifts and escalators.

Lastly, at the beginning of the 80s, certain city centres [Central Business Districts (CBD) in the United States] installed systems known as Downtown People Movers (DPM), which now constitute a fourth market for short-distance transport systems.

In greatly summarised form, this is the present situation to which we shall return in what follows.

2.2. An "interstitial" logic

It may appear at first surprising to see how little success the inventors' development efforts have had. Let us attempt an explanation. Summarising, our thesis is based on the idea that short-distance transport may be analysed as being the "missing links" in a public transport network in which there are local gaps. The role of such transport should therefore be understood in terms of an "interstitial" logic, the aim being to fill these gaps. We shall develop this argument in three different ways, to arrive at a positive conclusion on the consistency of future markets. Our basic idea is that these local gaps will be increasingly perceived by users in the future, for three reasons or logics.

2.2.1.   A logic based on the laws of speed: Bouladon

At the beginning of the 1970s, Gabriel Bouladon of the *Institut Batelle* in Geneva, developed his "General transport theory" (cf. Ref. 1).

77

Starting with considerations based on the theoretical constitution of the laws of door-to-door speed for the three major non-guided transport modes -- foot, car and plane -- Bouladon developed his famous theory of the two gaps or distances very poorly catered for by the public transport modes.

Without going into his argument in detail, Figure 1 clearly shows the result. A first "gap" appears for distances lying more or less between 400 and 2 000 metres. Why?

According to Bouladon, because, due to the rules which determine the mesh size of the conventional transport systems (such as bus or metro), access and waiting times cause people to prefer the car; but over such short distances the car is scarcely any better than public transport because there is, again, access time and then the problem of finding a parking spot.

With hindsight, we can now make many criticisms of this theory (so characteristic of the period!). The most important in our view is the under-estimation of the role of two-wheelers. A second criticism is that the theory implicitly considers that the different transport modes compete over an axis. This simplification, necessary to the theory, greatly limits its heuristic value, because the morphology of the mobility matrix to be served plays a role in the genesis of technical systems. We shall return to this point.

Bouladon's theory also has the merit, however, of highlighting the fact that it is because of the question of waiting time that the conventional public transport modes do not meet the requirements of short-distance mobility, and this problem is aggravated as the network mesh size gets larger.

In the words of Bouladon himself (*op. cit.* p. 26 and 27):

"Discontinuous public transport is therefore stuck between average speeds which are too low, if one opts for the fine mesh users want and access times which are too long, if one takes a greater mesh in the hope of attaining acceptable transport speeds (e.g. RER). Unfortunately, the stated speeds will not be those at which the public travel but merely those for the conveyance itself -- which is a poor consolation!

In conclusion, we can say that continuous transport alone gives us an economically viable solution to the problem of mass transport over short distances, where the reduction of access time is more important than the maximum speed obtained. Even if access time is zero, care must be taken to ensure that both access to the system and exit from it are easy operations.

In a nutshell, the system planned must fit in harmoniously with progress on foot, so as to retain some of the versatility and flexibility of walking. The ideal would be a system where one could walk as well, entering and leaving it at will; a velocity of from 10 to 15 km/h would be sufficient."

2.2.2.   Interconnection of the "major networks"

In another part of his pioneering work, Bouladon highlights a phenomenon which is not without its impact on the need for short-distance transport: the growing demands of high-speed transport users regarding the speed of transfer between links in their transport chain.

Three major fields of development in short-distance transport obviously respond to this logic.

First, the people-movers in airports, whose function is, among others, to enable air passengers to rapidly reach either a car park or a station of the regional public transport system linking them with the city centre.

Second, the big mainline stations, revitalised by the advent of high-speed trains, which of course have to be linked to the regional and urban networks.

Lastly, the rapid regional networks themselves (such as the RER) which, because of the sheer physical size of their interchange stations, will probably in the future constitute a particular market (for example, we shall be following with interest the project for public transport feeders in the Paris region and the complex design of its interchange stations with the radial lines of the urban and regional networks).

2.2.3.   Megaprojects "on the architectural scale"

Here again, over the past twenty years or so, two phenomena have been reinforcing one another and creating conditions favouring the opening up of new markets.

First, increasingly powerful private promoters have been taking charge of multifunctional projects associating offices, shops and dwellings on a scale which is "intermediate" from the transport standpoint. They are too small for the conventional public transport network to be able to satisfy their requirements for mobility and internal unity, too big for people not to seek the aid of mechanical transport.

This logic, more institutional than technical, is very present in the Paris region too. To cite but one (recent) example, the first ideas put forward in the context of the development project to replace the now defunct Renault plant at Boulogne-Billancourt, stress the need to equip the site with one or two short-distance transport systems. This seems to be a process which is to be found on several other sites in the region, for it is very much bound up with the size of the project (to give an idea, let us say about fifty hectares, but it may apply to projects covering from about twenty to one hundred hectares).

*
*   *

We thus see that a certain number of major trends in society and in urban development appear to be operating in favour of the development of short-distance transport. Let us now examine the morphological and technical families which are present on this market.

3. MORPHOLOGICAL AND TECHNICAL FAMILIES

3.1. Morphological families

It seems to us that we can better understand the disparate world of short-distance transport if we look at it in terms of a morphological structure, established first in the form of a mobility matrix and then in terms of the form of the technical response. We propose a conceptual framework based on three keywords, in increasing order of complexity for the system designer: **axis, loop and zone**.

a) The axial family

In this first family, the mobility matrix for movements on foot can be represented as follows:

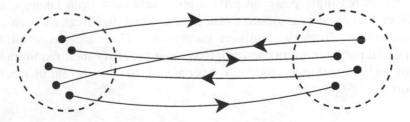

In other words, a concentrated zone of origins and destinations has to be linked over a short distance with another similar zone in such a way that with very short walking distances the user may access a point-to-point transport system over an axis.

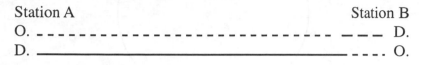

This family is particularly important because it is found very often in cases where the short-distance transport system is interconnected upstream and downstream with major transport chains.

b) The loop family

A second family, more difficult to interpret, concerns cases where the pedestrian mobility matrix is "multipolar" and can be served by a loop.

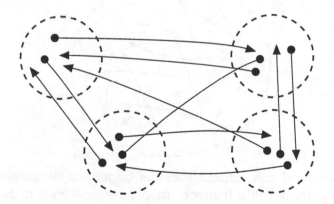

Here, concentrated zones of origins and destinations can be served "in a loop" without this arrangement causing unacceptable loss of time (thanks to the short distances involved). This is particularly important in the case of one-way loops. This configuration is found (frequently) in airports, theme parks and in a few city centres in the United States. In this last case they are known as Downtown People Movers (DPM) and these are discussed further below.

81

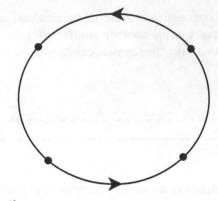

c) The zonal family

A recent apparition, the zonal family, covers cases where, in a restricted area inaccessible to the private car (and possibly two-wheelers), an attempt is made to serve a **homogeneous zonal matrix** of origins and destinations.

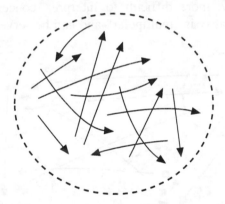

The absence of concentrated zones of origin and destination makes the conventional forms of public transport inappropriate and leads to the idea of cars available to all (a kind of ultra-simplified car hire with very numerous access points).

3.2. Technical families

3.2.1. Axial systems

a) Introduction

The idea of covering short distances between two points by sophisticated mechanical means generally leads to one of three types of solution:

1. **Continuous** transport, which includes constant speed and variable speed conveyors (high- speed moving pavements);

2. **Semi-continuous** transport, derived from a principle widely used in mountain transport, which consists of combining continuous or virtually continuous operation with stops (by means of cars moving at low speed along a platform) with conventional discontinuous operation between stations;

3. **Discontinuous** transport, in which a distinction can be made between systems with reversible vehicles and those with non-reversible vehicles. For short distances, reversibility has many advantages, notably in what are known as "funiculars" which enable two vehicles to operate without danger on a single track (except at the central crossing point, of course, where there is a double track).

These three families obviously each have their advantages and their disadvantages. In this chapter, without examining them exhaustively, we compare them mainly from the standpoint of two essential characteristics of any transport system:

-- The "entry-exit time" for the user;
-- The transport capacity as a function of the dimensions.

In practice, of course, a third essential characteristic of the system -- the cost -- would have to be taken into account.

b) The question of entry-exit time

Here, we refer to a conveyor belt of length L. We call the entry-exit time (**Tes**) for the conveyor, the time necessary to cover the distance separating a boarding point from an alighting point.

In this case, it will comprise:

-- An **access time** (obviously linked to the average waiting time) **Ta**;
-- A **vehicle time** (which depends on the movement of the vehicle) **Tv**;
-- An **exit time** (which depends on the average distance to be covered on foot between the exit door and the end of the platform CDD. This time is to be taken into consideration above all in the case of long trainsets) **Ts**:

$$Tes = Ta + Tv + Ts$$

By using a certain number of hypotheses to be found in Reference 2, it is possible to compare the performances of the three families on the basis of Figure 2.

Figure 2 shows the main fields of use for each of the three families:

-- High-speed conveyors give the shortest entry-exit times in the range from 100 to 200 metres. The field of use can obviously be extended beyond this limit, say, to about 300 metres because, for these distances, the loss of time caused by the use of the conveyor is limited.

The graph clearly shows, on the other hand, the risk that would be involved in the use of one or more high-speed conveyors over longer distances. It would appear that beyond 500 metres, the advantages of the two other families are so great that the conveyor can no longer be considered.

-- Cable cars (Vmax of about 10 m/s) are slightly less efficient than semi-continuous systems, but the difference is not very noticeable up to a distance of about one kilometre. Over short distances (300-1 000 m) which seem to constitute the ideal distance for cable systems, competition with semi-continuous transport is generally in terms of capacity, differences in the time performance not being significant. The situation is different over longer distances (1 000-2 000 m), where semi-continuous systems gradually gain the advantage in both entry-exit times and capacity.

-- All cable systems, which we assume to be limited to 10 m/s, are out-performed, as regards entry-exit time, by fast self-propelled vehicles (Vmax approximately 20 m/s) once the distance between stations exceeds 500 metres. Self-propelled vehicles are also superior to cable systems (given equivalent unit volumes of vehicles or trainsets) in terms of capacity under the above conditions. Cable systems, of course, still have a specific advantage in the case of sloping sites where the slope is steep enough to call for the use of rack and pinion (limit depending on the site and the climate, but in the range of 10-20 per cent).

c) The question of capacities

The curves, showing the hourly capacity in one direction at the intermediate stations, may be drawn for the cars, a type of system marked, it will be recalled, by a hyperbolic capacity law of the following type:

$$\text{Hourly capacity} = \frac{3600 \times CU}{I}$$

where: CU = Unit capacity of the trainset (number of passengers);
        I = Average interval between departures (second).

Using various hypotheses, also to be found in [2], we find the capacities of the families over an axis are as shown in Figure 3.

Comparison of the capacities calls for the following comments:

-- The capacities provided by systems of the "level funicular" type decrease very rapidly with distance (hyperbolic law);
-- Increasing the maximum speed from 10 m/s to 20 m/s has a very significant effect on capacity once the distance exceeds 500 metres;
-- The high-speed conveyor, with a capacity of 8 to 12 000 p/h, out-performs small cars (CU = 50 and 100 p) from the capacity standpoint, but is out-performed by a 200-passenger car up to about 300 metres and is then more or less equal to this car for distances greater than 300 metres;
-- The semi-continuous system, which provides a capacity of 4-5 000 p/h, regardless of the distance, is slightly superior to a car of 50 places over short distances (200 metres) and is equivalent to cars with 100 places between 500 and 800 metres (depending on the maximum speeds of these cars) and to cars with 200 places between 1 200 and 2 000 metres.

The advantage of the semi-continuous system over cars is the maintenance of good capacity with small vehicles over longer distances. The disadvantage is obviously that they impose a double track over the whole of the line, though the necessary width is not so great and the overhead structures are, in principle, lighter than in the case of shuttle cars of the same flow.

d) Factors affecting the feasibility of axial systems

Two types of consideration seem to be determinant for the feasibility of short-distance transport systems. The first is connected with the difficulties of construction and insertion, these two problems being indissociable. The second relates to the cost. We adopt a very cautious approach, citing only certain "orders of magnitude", notably for costs. It appears difficult, in fact, to give costs which can be generalised in the case of systems in which each site imposes its own particular type of insertion and construction.

The following table shows the orders of magnitude for the civil engineering costs of the two systems existing in practice (the high-speed conveyor being at present dormant, it is scarcely possible to cite any representative costs). The costs shown are taken from a recent study[6].

Table 1. **Total cost approached for a station and 400 metres of line**

Technique	Overhead	Underground	
		Cut and cover	Tunnelling machine
High-speed conveyor	15 MF	no reference	no reference
Semi-continuous	18 to 20 MF	30 to 45 MF	80 to 100 MF
Level funicular	25 to 35 MF	50 to 70 MF	120 to 150 MF

The important thing to note here is that the civil engineering costs for such systems are limited for sites where overhead installation is possible, but become much higher where the site imposes cut and cover or tunnelling techniques.

The costs of the vehicles and of the "system" proper are even more difficult to present, experience still being so limited and the cases so specific. If we take the semi-continuous family, it can be seen that the cost of a system offering a capacity of some 4 000 p/h can at present be estimated as being in the range of 20 to 60 MF per km. It should be noted that the cost varies very greatly, notably as a function of the level of comfort demanded.

This very rapid analysis of the feasibility of these systems thus reveals that it appears very largely dependent on the possibility of building an overhead system, which obviously depends very much on the type of location, as we try to show in Table 2.

Table 2. **Feasibility of overhead short-distance transport systems**

Location	European towns	US (or Asian) towns
City centre systems	Extremely rare	Fairly frequently possible in CBD
Systems for transfers between land transport modes	Extremely rare, the stations usually being in densely built-up areas	Possible in certain cases
Airport systems	Very often possible	Very often possible
Systems for theme parks (or international exhibitions)	Always possible (inconceivable otherwise)	Always possible (inconceivable otherwise)

-- Operating costs

It is difficult to give estimates of the operating costs of these transport systems. They depend to an enormous extent on the quality requirements imposed in each case by the client and by the degree of "toughness" of the environment, notably in terms of vandalism.

We limit ourselves to giving some orders of magnitude for the full-time staff employed on certain projects enumerated in an article by D.J. Ochsner and H. Huyn (in Ref. 3). These figures suffice to show that total automation, although absolutely essential, does not constitute a radical solution to the problem posed for these short-distance transport systems by the extensive maintenance and operating tasks and the resulting costs.

Table 3. **Personnel employed on different projects**

Airport or Town	Operating staff				Vehicle-miles per year
	Adminis-tration	Operation	Mainten-ance	Total	
Airports:					
Dallas	2	16	83	101	3 400 000
Atlanta	9	18	30	57	1 050 000
Tampa	2	3	12	17	650 000
Orlando	1	4	11	16	650 000
Gatwick	2	3	16	21	595 000
Chicago	2	13	44	59	715 000
Morgantown	11	14	39	64	801 000	
Detroit	8	16	39	63	57 000 ?
Miami	6	10	32	48	427 000
Jacksonville	1	2	4	7	66 000
Harbour Is.	-	1	3	4	72 000
Las Colinas	1	4	8	13	262 000 *

* This figure must be a forecast: the actual figures are very much lower.

We note that systems with passive vehicles, using cables, often admittedly only running over very short distances, appear to require considerably less maintenance staff, in the present state of the art, than systems with active vehicles. But it should be noted that certain costs incurred by cable systems cannot appear directly in these comparisons of staff numbers (replacement of the cable after some years of operation, inspection of the safety devices by outside staff, etc.).

The above figures must therefore be used with caution.

To conclude this section on costs, we would say that one of the major problems with short-distance transport systems is indisputably their overall technical immaturity. We are not thinking of any system in particular, of course, but simply pointing out the difficulty of keeping to reasonable operating costs for systems still marked by the embryonic nature of the corresponding "markets". We can hope for an improvement in the future, though with a very big question mark (outside the airports and theme parks) due to the spread of vandalism in our urban societies, which, it must be admitted, are full of tensions.

This is a general problem, of course, but it is particularly acute in the case of these small automated systems which are always somewhat more fragile than the conventional heavier systems.

3.2.2.   Loop systems

We have seen above that in certain cases a multipolar logic could lead the promoters of short-distance transport systems to propose loop systems. We distinguish between three fields of application here.

a)   Theme parks and exhibitions

Here the loop configuration is almost the rule. It is, in fact, natural to seek a configuration making it possible to "do the rounds" of the attractions of the park, generally on a one-way loop. The time loss involved with a one-way system is not a major problem on these sites and the construction costs and problems of insertion are reduced. Some forty sites have been equipped with very simple systems, often inspired by urban monorails, but lighter. Half of these sites operate permanently (Disneyworld and similar) and the other half consists of installations in some of the many international fairs and exhibitions held over the past forty years or so. The market is, for the most part, split between two manufacturers. The great majority of sites are equipped by Habegger-Von Roll (light monorails), others by AEG-Westinghouse (model C-100 or similar).

We recall the existence of these many "leisure" systems because, though they lie outside the main field of interest of this report, their industrial importance needs to be highlighted, as it is considerable for the sector.

b) Urban complexes

Going a step further in ambition, we find loop systems serving suburban areas close to metro or RER stations, and used for both internal circulation and as feeders. The most striking examples are to be found in Japan and the United States (we have limited ourselves to loops with a total line length of less than five kilometres).

The following table summarises the characteristics of the different systems. It should be pointed out that they are discontinuous and traditional.

Table 4. **Characteristics of different systems**

Town	Length (km)	Number of stations	Number of vehicles	Capacity (pass/h.)
Kobe (Japan)	6.4	9	12 x 6	10 000
Sakura (Japan)	4.1	6	?	2 600
Ôsaka (Japan)	6.6	8	12 x 6	5 000
Las Colinas (USA)	4.8*	4	4	Very low

* Present configuration.

We have ridership figures for two of these systems. In Kobe, the Port-Liner ridership has stabilized at some 40 000 passengers a day, which is very satisfactory for a system of this configuration.

In Las Colinas, on the other had, the operation would appear to be a failure. The system operates regularly for only two hours a day (and on demand the rest of the time, which is a world first) Ridership is in the order of 2 700 passengers a week. It is difficult to understand what could have inspired this project, which is apparently incoherent.

c) Central Business Districts

A third and last field in which loop systems have been installed is that of Central Business Districts. In this case the genesis of the systems (essentially American) is highly complex. We summarise it by recalling three historical factors:

-- First, the will of the UMTA to equip the towns of the United States with highly efficient public transport systems (a will expressed as early as the end of the 60s);

-- Second, the proliferation of ambitions and technological research (and disappointments) into a concept as attractive as it was unrealistic: Personal Rapid Transit (PRT). The original idea was to combine the advantages of public and private transport through providing small cars on a light and meshed infrastructure, permitting changes of line without a change of vehicle and thus giving a virtually door-to-door service;

-- Finally, the desire of the US administration to show some positive result, even if only limited, from this largely unfruitful technological research, led to the launching of a national development programme in 1976.

A few towns were then attracted by the quite exceptional levels of subsidy offered by the Federal Government. After some hesitation, three towns decided to embark on the construction of Downtown People Movers, which can thus be regarded as the final offspring of research and development which had been going on for almost twenty-five years. These towns were Detroit, Miami and Jacksonville.

It would appear that the concept of Downtown People Movers has not found many emulators outside the United States. There is the case of Sydney, Australia, which is close in spirit to the American DPM (loop linking development areas in town centres marked by a certain economic and social decomposition). There is, however, a very big difference in the cost of the operation: while the United States projects turned out to be veritable bottomless pits financially, every effort was made to save money on the Australian project. It has, in fact, attracted a great deal of criticism on environmental grounds.

Table 5. **Characteristics of different systems**

Town	Length of system (loop) in km	Number of stations	Number of vehicles	Clientele (order of magnitude per day)	Cost (in MMD)
Miami	3.2	9	12	10 000	160
Detroit	4.7*	13	13	10 000	200
Jacksonville	1.1**	3	2	1 800	35
Sydney	3.6	7	6 x 7	?	low

*   One-way operation.
**   The system is to be extended.

One can but be struck by the modest ridership of these Downtown People Movers.

To what do we attribute what looks very much like a failure? For some commentators, the situation of the CBD, notably in Detroit and Miami, is too run-down for public transport to be able to play any locomotive role. It is also pointed out that insecurity, whether real or simply perceived, can play a strong dissuasive role. Lastly, it is worthwhile recalling that, of course, nothing has been done to restrict the use of the car, the greatly dominant mode (notably thanks to the fact that all the city centre buildings have big private car parks, often free).

Summing up, there is no reason to believe that it would be desirable to transpose these American experiments to Europe, and there are in fact no serious projects of this type to report.

3.2.3.   *Zonal systems*

When the mobility matrix cannot be reduced to a line or a loop, hope is naturally placed in individual "instant car hire" systems. Such systems were experimented with unsuccessfully during the 70s in Montpellier (Procotip) and Amsterdam (Witcars).

The concept behind these systems is to allow the users to use a fleet of small vehicles available in a great many car parks in the zone concerned, through a system of electronic access, automatically performing all the commercial operations involved in car hire (identification of the hirer, charging, etc.).

91

The idea is attractive. It is at present being revived in France in the hope that it may serve as a vector for the introduction of the electric car. However, quite apart from the problems connected with the economics of the electric vehicle, there are a good many other difficulties which we briefly summarise below:

-- Coverage of the zone by a sufficient number of car parks;
-- Access possible or not for non-residents;
-- Relations with taxi owners;
-- Dynamic adjustment of the fleet between the various car parks;
-- Careless use and/or vandalism;
-- Size effect (what minimum fleet is required to make the system attractive?);
-- Charging system (per km, per hour, etc.);
-- General image (is it sufficiently acceptable on social grounds?) and the problem of possible subsidies; etc.

Time will tell whether these ideas have a better chance of coming to fruition in the 90s or 2000s than in the 70s. Our own forecast is very cautious, not to say reserved, unless car hire firms and taxi owners themselves adopt the idea in order to make it live and prosper. For the moment, however, it is mainly the public transport operators who are interested in it, which is necessary but, in our opinion, not sufficient.

4. THE OUTLOOK: ELEMENTS FOR A DISCUSSION

4.1. Market prospects

In this section we break down the market, or field of application, into four segments: airports, theme parks and exhibitions, big rail interchanges and, lastly, megaprojects on the architectural scale.

Before dealing with these subjects, however, we should recall a few general factors which merit examination:

-- *The general economic situation and the short-distance transport market*

Here there are generally two conflicting theses. The first, pessimistic, stresses the non-essential nature of many short-distance transport projects. As a result, it expects such projects to be dropped in periods of economic recession. The second thesis, optimistic, uses a different argument: development bodies, public or private, should in lean periods be inclined to bank on inter-modality, implementing lighter and more local projects. This mechanism, if it materialised, would thus work in favour of short-distance transport. We leave it to the reader to form his own opinion.

-- *Growing interest in the environment and the short-distance transport market*

Here again, there are two conflicting theses. The first, more general, starts with the idea that growing concern with the environment is favourable to the development of public transport, and notably rail transport. This development of public transport in general, in a world concerned with comfort and subject to the attraction of the private car, can but lead to a very strong desire to improve interchange facilities. This would therefore logically lead to a growing market for short-distance transport technologies.

The second, more specific, is based more on the observation already made in this report which very closely associates the feasibility of short-distance transport projects with the possibility of building overhead infrastructures and thus avoiding the very high costs of underground construction. From this standpoint, the growing concern with local environmental values can play a very negative role by opposing any overhead project where there are frontages (which amounts to a virtual ban on overhead projects outside airports and theme parks, except perhaps in totally new urban developments).

-- *Automatic ticketing and the development of short-distance transport*

The development of automatic ticketing should be a basic factor very favourable to short-distance transport. It now seems that the time has gone when such installations could be provided without charge in urban applications. Conventional ticketing is often difficult to arrange economically for these systems, however, and modern electronic methods of payment may be a very useful way of resolving this type of problem in the future.

-- *Metropolisation and the development of short-distance transport*

In our view, the "metropolisation" mechanism in Europe, i.e. the concentration of populations into certain big conurbations of several million people, is favourable to the development of short-distance transport. Virtually all the French projects, to take but this example, are concentrated in the Paris region.

Let us now examine the factors specific to the four "market segments".

a)   Airport people-movers

This market is and, in our opinion, will remain the biggest. Here a factor for development seems to us to be the deregulation of air transport which leads to the phenomenon of "hubbing" and the virtually explosive growth in traffic in the biggest airports. According to a recent study by *Aéroports de Paris*, the mere growth of the aircraft parking areas could lead the majority of airports handling 25 million passengers a year (Pax) to install such systems in the future.

Of the twenty-two airports handling 20 million Pax in 1992, about ten are already equipped or are about to be, eight others are intensively studying their project and only four appear to be uninterested. Of the thirty-two airports with a traffic of between 10 MPax and 20 MPax, just under ten are already equipped or about to be and as many again are at present intensively studying projects.

These figures put the airport market segment very far ahead of any of the other foreseeable markets, with perhaps one or two major projects per year over the next ten years. Only an even bigger air transport crisis than the present one could modify this favourable outlook.

b)   Theme parks and exhibitions

It is much more difficult to make a forecast for this tourism-leisure field. The recent problems of many theme parks in France augurs ill for any great opportunities in Europe, at any rate nothing comparable with what has happened in the United States, where some twenty systems are in operation, as we have said.   There remain the big international exhibitions, which will continue of course at the rate of, roughly, one or two every ten years.

This is undoubtedly the field where the effect of the general economic situation most clearly plays a role. If "American-style" mass tourism in fact develops, it is in our opinion in the context of a very consumption-oriented society, with relative prosperity for the population categories most attracted by theme parks (young couples with children belonging to the lower-middle social classes).

Lastly, it should be pointed out that certain theme parks, even among the biggest (EuroDisney, for example), have not installed any of the systems we are concerned with.

c) Major rail interchanges and feeder services

The gradual establishment of a large high-speed rail network in Europe should lead to new short-distance transport requirements, due to the effect of two complementary trends.

First, the size and location of HST stations are such that the distances to be covered when changing line or mode are increasingly long. Second, passengers cannot understand why, after an extremely rapid and comfortable intercity journey, they should lose in terms of wasted time and discomfort in transferring to the urban network all that they have previously gained. The example of the *Gare Montparnasse* in Paris is a perfect illustration of this phenomenon.

In the longer term, it is now envisaged to complement the bus feeder services existing for the major stations of the regional express network (RER) by short-distance transport lines. One site is already equipped in this way in the Paris region (Noisy-le-Grand) and projects are well advanced at several others (Créteil, Charenton, etc.).

It is the existence of this potential market which justifies the growing interest of the traditional network operators (notably the RATP) in certain specialised techniques (notably SK).

d) Megaprojects on the architectural scale

This is a final field in which a certain number of projects may see the light of day, once the present property crisis is over, of course.

As we have already pointed out, public and private promoters often find advantage in developing megaprojects in very close liaison with the public transport network, but because of their sheer size such projects sometimes make it necessary to have an internal short-distance transport system.

This type of development is still rare but could come about in the case of certain "prestigious" sites (in France, Boulogne-Billancourt, extension of La Défense, etc.).

In conclusion, let us note the existence, still to be confirmed, of certain possibilities in the hospitals sector.

4.2. A developing sector, finally escaping from industrial immaturity?

Taking all uses together, it can be seen that the market for mechanised transport over short distances remains narrow, characterised by a "business turnover" of just one or two systems a year on average, to give an order of magnitude, in all the industrialised countries.

This is why in previous studies we had preferred to speak of opportunity for development rather than market, a term which too much implies a possible reproducibility of the systems.

The present rate of implementations is a little too low to give manufacturers conditions which would lead to the emergence of standard, reproducible system components which could bring, if not series effects which are improbable, at least a positive effect of accumulation of know-how.

Only two manufacturers, one in the United States and the other in Switzerland, have succeeded (on the airport and leisure markets, respectively) in reaching this almost industrial stage: AEG-Westinghouse, with its C-100 systems installed in some fifteen airport sites; Habegger-Von Roll, with its monorails on some ten "leisure" sites. Behind them, two French and one American manufacturer are neck-and-neck, with just a few installations (Matra, Soulé, Otis). They, of course, hope to be able to substantially improve this situation, and in our view have a good chance of success, each having opted for different and therefore complementary technologies.

Behind this trio, as can be seen in the Annex, lies the vast field of local experimentation, more or less successful but not reproduced, with little industrial impact in the best of cases, often unfavourable and sometimes catastrophic in others.

We are therefore inclined to conclude this discussion on a note of qualified optimism:

1. **Affirming the existence of growing outlets**, at least in the airports and the articulations of the rail networks in the major cities;

2. **Expressing the wish to see a certain "fixing" of the technologies** so that real industrial competence can be developed in this field. It is, in fact, a still marginal but important matter to improve the public transport supply in the cities of Europe (and, why not, the world), which are laying ever greater emphasis on the importance of intermodality in their policies.

FIGURES

Figure 1. Gap zones (partly covered by public transport modes)

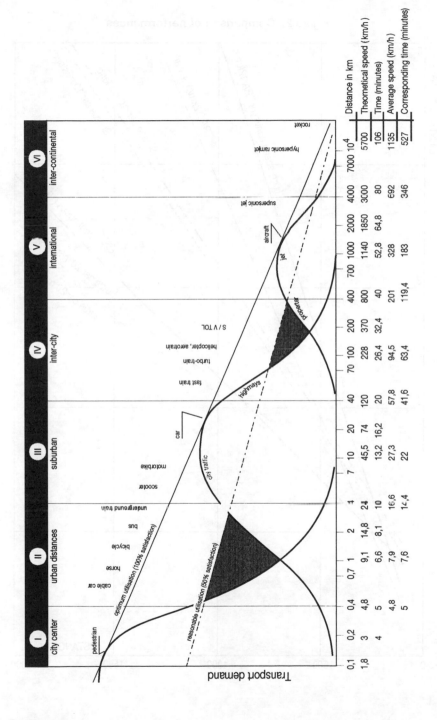

Source : Rapport OCDE (Réf. 1)

Figure 2. **Comparison of performances**

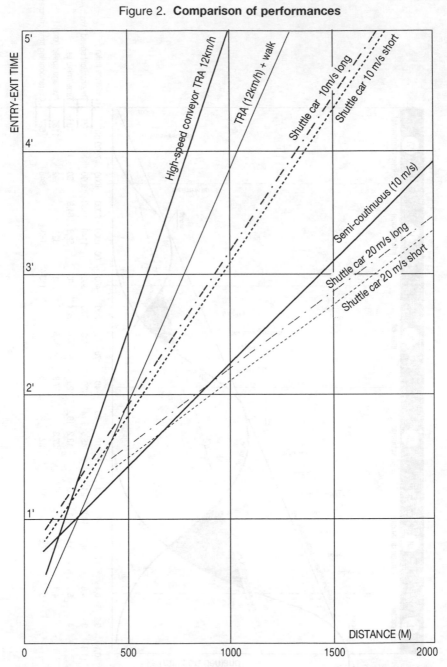

Figure 3. **Capacity of straight line people movers as a function of station distances, unit capacity and maximum speed of vehicles**

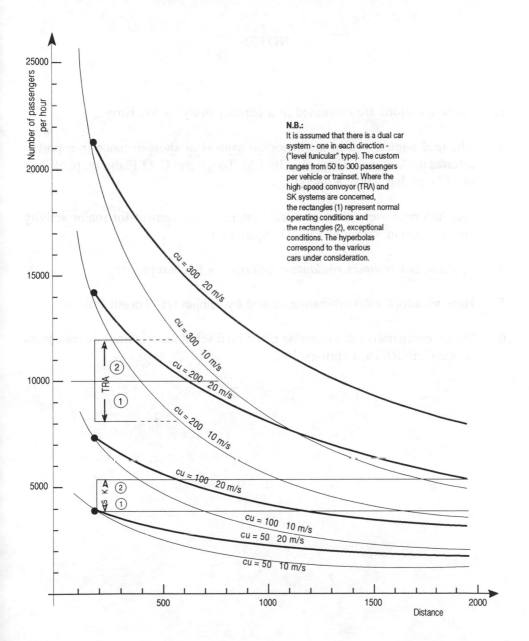

N.B.:
It is assumed that there is a dual car system - one in each direction - ("level funicular" type). The custom ranges from 50 to 300 passengers per vehicle or trainset. Where the high-speed convoyor (TRA) and SK systems are concerned, the rectangles (1) represent normal operating conditions and the rectangles (2), exceptional conditions. The hyperbolas correspond to the various cars under consideration.

NOTES

1. These questions are discussed in a parallel study by W. Brög.

2. The reader interested in the historical aspects of short-distance transport is referred to *Passenger Conveyor*, by J.M. Tough and C. O'Flaherty, published in 1971 by Ian Allan, London.

3. "An historical view of mechanical systems of movement for major activity centres", Brian Richards, OECD, April 1970.

4. P. Patin, *Les trottoirs roulants accélérés*, La Recherche.

5. Here we adopt a denomination coined by Fabian (cf. Transit Pulse).

6. "Étude comparative des coûts de génie civil selon les systèmes de transports adoptés", INRETS, February 1992.

ANNEX

SHORT-DISTANCE TRANSPORT SYSTEMS

Category 1: Systems installed (and planned) on several sites

• WESTINGHOUSE C-100	Different countries -- mainly USA
• OTIS - (Cable) -- Air Metro	"
• MATRA -- VAL 206 and VAL 256	"
• VON ROLL -- Various monorails	"
• SOULE -- SK (various names)	Various countries -- mainly France
• UTDC	United States and Canada
• WEDWAY	United States

For the record:

• Multiple speed conveyors (historical) United States and France;
• Conventional funiculars.

Category 2: Systems built for a specific site, now in service but not reproduced

• AIRTRANS	Dallas Airport	USA
• OTIS (LIM)	Duke Hospital	USA
• H-BAHN	Dortmund University	FRG
• POMA 2000	Laon	F
• CABINEN-TAXI	Ziegenheim Hospital	FRG
• MAGLEV G.E.C.	Birmingham Airport	UK
• WESTINGHOUSE C45	Las Colinas	USA
• FORD ACT	Dearborn, Michigan	USA
• BOEING PRT	Morgantown	USA
• KAWASAKI	Kobe	JAPAN
• NIIGATA-VOUGHT	Osaka	JAPAN

Category 3: **Systems intensively studied, as far as "life-size" prototype, with simulation or initial use, then abandoned:**

• NEVER STOP RAILWAY	(historical)	UK
• SPEEDAWAY	Dunlop-Battelle	CH
• TELECANAPE	Habegger	CH
• TELERAIL	Neyrpic	F
• TRAX	ACB-RATP	F
• ARAMIS	MATRA-RATP	F
• C-BAHN	MBB-Demag-Hagen	FRG
• M. BAHN	Berlin-Brunswick	FRG
• POMA SC	Grenoble	F
• VEC	Parking FNAC-Paris	F
• DELTA V	BLM Nantes	F
• TELEBUS	Guimbal-St. Etienne	F
• KAWASAKI	KCV-Kakogawa	JAPAN

Note: This list does not claim to be exhaustive. It should be completed by **some sixty purely industrial projects** not having reached the stage mentioned in Category 3, and a few Asian (Japan) and South American (Brazil) projects with which the author is not familiar but which are apparently without any great impact on the industrial scene.

SELECT BIBLIOGRAPHY

1. OECD (1970), "Systèmes de transport pour les pôles d'activité", Groupe consultatif sur la recherche en matière de transport, Deuxième examen d'évaluation technologique, April.

2. Bieber, A. *et al.* (1986), "Comparaison des systèmes de transport hectométrique", Synthèse n° 1, INRETS, Arcueil, April.

3. Bondada, M.V.A., W.J. Sproule and E.S. Neumann (eds.) (1989), *Automated People Movers I and II*, Proceedings of the First and Second Conference, 1985 and 1989, Miami, Florida. ASCE, New York.

4. Lea, N.D. and SNV (1983), *International Transit Compendium*, Vol. IV, No. 1, Automated Guideway Transit, Washington-Hamburg.

5. INRETS-CRESTA (1992), "Étude comparative des coûts de génie civil selon les systèmes de transports adoptés", pour le compte de l'AFME. Lille, February.

6. RATP-DEV (1992), "Systèmes automatiques de transport de voyageurs aux USA", Mission report, June.

7. Fabian, J.L. (ed.), *Transit Pulse Review*, Boston, USA, various issues.

8. Scherrer, M. (1992), *Systèmes de transport et Aéroports*, Aéroports de Paris DIN, September.

9. Soulas, C., "Automated guideway transit systems and Personal rapid transit systems", in Papageorgiou, M. (ed.), *Concise Encyclopedia of Traffic and Transportation Systems*, Pergamon Press.

10. Fabian, J.L. (1990), "Airport People Movers: Reaching outside the fence", *Journal of Advanced Transportation, Vol. 24*, No. 3.

11. INRETS-CRESTA (1992), "Nouvelles technologies et perspectives des transports pour villes moyennes", Journée d'étude, Lille, 12th June.

12. INRETS, "New developments of guided transport in Europe", in: Soulas, C. (ed.), *Journal of Advanced Transportation, Special Issue.* To be published.

13. "New transport systems in the world", (1979) in: Tsukio, Yoshio and Brian Richards (eds.), *Process Architecture*, No. 9, Tokyo.

14. CETUR-DTT, Ministère des Transports (1988), *Matériels français de transports collectifs urbains*, May.

15. Tough, J.M. and C. O'Flaherty (1971), *Passenger Conveyors*, Ian Allan, London.

16. Patin, P. (1980), *Les trottoirs roulants accélérés*, La Recherche, Paris.

SUMMARY OF DISCUSSIONS

SUMMARY

1. NON-MOTORISED URBAN TRAVEL

As noted at the start of the Round Table, many routine trips are made on foot. However, it can be said that perceptions are subjective, i.e. that they do not reflect reality, for when designing urban areas, planners underestimate the number of trips on foot and the possibility of non-motorised transport. Owing to the policies which have been continually adopted for urban areas, citizens are now very critical about transport planning, precisely because it does not provide sufficient scope for non-motorised transport.

The situation admittedly varies from country to country, but for the time being planning is still very often focused on economically active males, who prefer driving, and has gone a long way to meeting their demands. On the other hand, planners have underestimated the volume of journeys on foot and quite often ignored the potential use of the bicycle. Recent changes, however, particularly with the extension of pedestrian zones in town centres, have resulted in less motorised transport. The long-term trend nevertheless shows an increase in the use of private cars and a decline in journeys on foot. It is the considerable development of motorised transport that has shaped the trend in mobility.

Another point to be noted is that times tend to remain constant and that trips in urban areas are usually over short distances. The car is thus often used for short trips, particularly within major towns. Broadly speaking, moreover, it may be pointed out that there has been little change in the needs that mobility caters for, more particularly occupational and shopping requirements.

Owing to congestion in urban areas, it can be said that the car saves little time compared with the bicycle. Surveys have shown that the majority of car trips in urban areas do not exceed five kilometres, which means that the car is not essential even if it is frequently used. Since in most cases the driver is not carrying anything in his car, alternatives to its use can be considered. According to traffic studies, the use of the private car can now be reduced by about 15 to 20 per cent. The Round Table participants thus concluded that the unwillingness to use alternatives to the private car would have to be overcome. At present, citizens and policy decisionmakers alike think that the private car must take a less important place, and each of them points a finger at the other, although both should take a different approach: the policymaker by influencing transport planning and the citizen by not using his car when he can do without it. Whether the decisionmaker be policymaker or citizen, more attention obviously has to be given to non-motorised transport. Drastic action involving substantial investment is not necessary for this purpose. Changes can be expected simply from an awareness of the problem.

To start with, walking and cycling have to be considered in studies on mobility and on the general organisation of transport. It would be a serious mistake to omit these modes, but the complexity of possible developments must be remembered. For instance, an improvement in public transport may have a limited effect on travel by car but attract those who normally walk or cycle. Action must also be taken on urban design. The car has modified distances and behaviour in urban environments. Other ways of life have evolved with the greater distances between residential areas, shops and centres of economic activity. Now the aim is to build towns which keep distances short, whereas the private car has given rise to towns which require travel over long distances. In order to find out what the public wants, it would also be useful to know more about the motives for choosing particular modes. Clearly, an increase in transport distances prompts people to drive. Families who have opted for a house in the suburbs, will use their cars more frequently if public transport cannot be adapted to their needs. Transport times and distances are important factors in mobility. Motivation studies may also show that the private car is attractive in that it gives an impression of freedom and seems immune to insecurity risks.

In the United Kingdom, urban transport surveys have shown that high-frequency minibus services are a good alternative to walking and driving. These services are appreciated by elderly people for shopping, visits to local authority offices, their bank, etc. It is certain that, as people grow older, they prefer motorised transport for quite short distances, while in other age groups 30 per cent of journeys can take place on foot or by bicycle.

An aspect which should be considered is that women are now tending to respond in much the same way as men and, accordingly, they will drive if public transport is not convenient enough. Private car transport often seems attractive since transport times and costs by this mode are underestimated. In an urban area, average car speed is ten kilometres an hour, a speed possible on other modes, particularly the bicycle when special infrastructure has been provided. It must be admitted, however, that the co-existence of pedestrians, bicycles and private cars is a problem, so that a suitable type of infrastructure which does not give cars priority is needed. Broadly speaking, it seems that the private car can be replaced for short distances unless the geographical layout of both infrastructure and facilities is redesigned.

The Round Table specialists considered that the various sections of the community have to be persuaded that the car is not needed for some trips. More precisely, drivers can certainly do without their cars on various occasions during the week. This is practically impossible when the car is used for combined trips, such as taking the children to school before going to work. Disregarding such trips, for which it is difficult to imagine an alternative, surveys show that there is still a substantial number (about 20 per cent) of trips for which the private car is not necessary. This would cut down greatly on pollution, for it must be remembered that short drives in town when car engine temperatures are still low cause considerable pollution which is also detrimental to pedestrians and cyclists.

In a system where the private car and non-motorised means of transport co-exist, it has to be admitted that the private car is much safer than the bicycle. In fact, in an environment dominated by the private car, two-wheelers become a risky form of transport, even when they are not motorised. It is thus essential to improve infrastructure by providing cycle paths if the aim is to increase the use of ecological transport modes. On the other hand, when towns are built on steep slopes, it is more difficult to encourage cycling, and in such cases appropriate techniques, such as mechanised short-distance transport, must be provided for difficult stretches.

It is obvious that the morphological structure of a town, the trips generated by this structure and modal choices are interdependent, but certain basic trends applicable to practically every country must also be mentioned. One is the increase in income which makes it easier to purchase and run a private car. Another long-standing trend is the deliberate policy of developing road infrastructure. Together they are now generating external costs (noise, pollution, congestion) which are not paid for in full by users. The policy focus is therefore gradually turning to the promotion of alternative transport modes, as well as restrictions on private car travel, the main one being the probable introduction of road pricing, i.e. a toll system for congested urban areas. It must also be remembered that, as a result of urban sprawl, more and more trips are not to the town centre but between different outlying areas. In the absence of a satisfactory means of public transport, the car is used for these journeys. More attention will have to be given in the future to these flows in order to discourage the use of the private car.

2. MECHANISED SHORT-DISTANCE TRANSPORT

Mechanised short-distance transport is not a recent concern. Even before the start of the century, attempts were made to adapt public transport modes to the demand for short-distance trips, and services for distances between about 500 and 2 000 metres are still lacking. Metro and bus networks cater for demand for distances of two to three kilometres. With conventional vehicles, the networks are not yet sufficiently dense for short runs. There is also the question of frequency: on short distances, transport access times (walking and waiting) are prohibitive if passengers have a long wait, or if the distance between access points is too great.

Many researchers have tried out transport techniques in the course of time, but the results have been modest, whether in the case of high-speed moving pavements or small cabins permitting almost continuous operation. On the whole, few of the projects attracted any interest.

It should be understood that such systems are needed when there are gaps or missing links in transport chains. These systems are to be found in stations, airports and major architectural projects or in recent mixed systems (air terminals, high-speed train, aircraft). They can be seen as an answer to an exceptional need caused by the lack of conventional public transport and by the impossibility of travelling by car, on foot or by bicycle. The pattern of the points to be served can be used to define different network forms, i.e. point to point, loop or zonal systems (see report by A. Bieber).

With the exception of the rapid development of airport facilities, the economic climate is not conducive to further investment in public transport for the time being. However, with the development of automatic ticketing, a contribution by the user to funding such infrastructure is conceivable. In any case, in the context of a comprehensive urban project, the facilities are not costly. It is more the fact that these urban projects have come to a halt which may lead to a slowdown in investment in mechanised short-distance transport.

If the ecological aspect is included, it can be seen that mechanised short-distance transport is complementary to public transport as it makes transfers more efficient. On the other hand, the viaducts that are often required create problems of an aesthetic nature. The ecological impact may therefore seem somewhat diminished but, as a result of the metropolisation trend and airport development, there are possibilities of bringing in motorised short-distance transport techniques. Owing to the increasing range of technologies, only a few techniques will in fact be selected and the number of systems produced will always be limited. It will therefore be difficult to write down industrial investment over such numbers, even if substantial needs can be foreseen between and within stations and airports.

Other uses of mechanical systems were cited at the Round Table, such as transport to the different parts of trade fairs, major tourist facilities and office complexes. Mechanical facilities in car parks for vertical and horizontal links with surface roads are also a possibility. For the time being, about fifty or so systems are operational in various parts of the world and they are used at airports, in theme parks and for architectural megaprojects. Other uses are conceivable with underground car parks and projects for underground motorways. In all cases, however, the scope for these short-distance transport systems is limited and they cannot replace walking or cycling. They must be seen as exceptional transport modes responding to special needs in specific environments.

In deciding where mechanised short-distance transport facilities can be used, it may be assumed that two types of urban context are concerned:

-- A long-established environment where public transport networks exist and where there is no need for mechanised modes as journeys can be made on foot;
-- A recent or predominantly concrete environment which has set limits to walking and cycling.

It is in the latter context that mechanised transport is needed. It is not certain, however, that the trend will continue with a further increase in major architectural projects at a time of crisis in the construction industry. In any event, the Round Table specialists pointed out that if contemporary architectural projects were well designed, there would be no need for auxiliary modes for distances of 500 to 2 000 metres. Obviously such journeys have always been made on foot. Moreover, walking can be made more pleasant by protecting pedestrians from bad weather. But when luggage has to be carried, mechanised short-distance transport may be appropriate. Such systems can also be used when passengers are kept waiting because public transport services are not frequent enough.

Little information is available on the costs of short-distance transport systems, but it can be assumed that if these investments are intended to ensure continuity in transport services, they are necessarily an asset for the complexes in which they are used. This may amply justify their existence and, moreover, private funding can be considered for their construction owing to progress in electronic funds transfer. These mechanised short-distance transport systems may also be used as feeder services for a metro network. Small branch lines would thus run from the dense segments of such a network. This scheme is not feasible in every case but may be suitable for certain architectural projects.

Some of the Round Table specialists considered that existing transport modes, such as buses or minibuses, could play the role expected of mechanical short-distance systems, as shown by some examples in the United States and the United Kingdom. The appropriate solution in fact depends on the topography of the areas to be served and probably on the applicable technologies as well. It was pointed out that short-distance mechanised transport systems are designed for use in a costly, high-technology environment and are suitable for major projects where the system costs can be internalised. They are practically never used in a specifically urban context, unless they serve major architectural projects. In such cases, the pricing problem does not arise since, when mechanised transport is integrated with a larger but closed entity, the lack of a specific tariff system does not matter. On the other hand, at sites which do not operate revenues, the tariff system is a problem. It is this factor which has so far prevented the development of short-distance projects in our cities. In fact, for the time being, a high-technology environment calls precisely for high-technology solutions for its complementary equipment. Some preference for the spectacular is perhaps not absent from certain projects. Another point is that urban transport facilities may be drawn into this technology race by the increased speed of intercity transport (high-speed rail, aircraft). In addition, although short-distance mechanised transport systems were initially simple and inexpensive, the technologies have become more complex and the scope for their use is limited to sufficiently high traffic volumes.

The fact remains that, quite often, mechanised short-distance transport operations are difficult to organise because they compete with journeys on foot, which cost nothing. Walking is possible only if there are no obstacles such as slopes or intersections. Everything suggests that there is an obvious need for mechanised transport in specific areas where various kinds of advanced technology co-exist.

3. INCENTIVES FOR THE USE OF "ECOLOGICAL" TRANSPORT MODES

The potential for any transfers from the private car to walking, cycling or public transport cannot be accurately assessed. All the various studies on the subject show that private car users do not realise or underestimate the possibilities of using alternative modes. The social costs of the private car can therefore be substantially reduced. However, the best approach in the long term is to base planning projects on the concept of compact towns. It is possible to restrict the use of private cars in the town centre and to provide car parks on the outskirts. Shops and offices located in the centre can be reached by public transport or other ecological modes. It is also possible to provide bicycles in the town parking areas and equip sites for cycling. On the other hand, access to all amenities by private car is not desirable, and it is preferable to ensure that the town centre has to be bypassed by cars going from one district to another. A formula of this kind has been successfully implemented in Gröningen and, after some misgivings, shopkeepers have come to appreciate its advantages. The overall concept may obviously seem costly, but it also shows the possibility of influencing individual choices and thereby reducing the use of the private car despite its positive image. Of all the possible measures, limited parking times in town centres always seem to have a deterrent effect on use of the car.

One obstacle which frequently stands in the way of a more receptive attitude to ecological transport modes is that the decisionmakers take some persuading. There is considerable agreement concerning these modes among transport specialists, but it has to be reflected in policy decisions which reject the traditional all-importance of the car. This is an imperative, even though the vast majority of people have access to a car. The decisions may therefore prove difficult to take, but attitudes are now in fact changing in this respect. What is important is that all transport modes should be incorporated from the start of the planning phase and that the private car should not interfere with public transport but serve rather as a complementary mode for long distances. Short-distance transport should therefore form part of a more comprehensive scheme which integrates the different modes and the specific contribution expected of them. The pervading atmosphere and safety aspects associated with alternative transport modes must also be considered if drivers are to be weaned away from the car.

At present the move is towards a series of measures to discourage driving, for the cost of running expenses of a car are still fairly low in that they do not cover the costs incurred as a result of pollution, the loss of time in traffic jams and the waste of energy. These car expenses can be increased within reasonable limits by taxes on fuel, parking or toll charges and road pricing. At the same time, investment in public transport and ecological alternatives is necessary if mobility is not to be restricted. Encouraging the use of electric minibuses, cycle paths, funiculars, etc. can be used as a basis for a policy seeking to replace the private car.

To obtain a better understanding of mobility and prepare decisions, studies and research covering every type of journey (by foot, bicycle, public transport and car) must be carried out. Better information on motives behind modal choice may also make the reasons for modal transfers clearer. In this context, users -- particularly elderly persons, women and children -- must be asked for their opinions. As far as possible, the planning scheme must avoid long transport distances to the public's usual destination points. This is possible only in towns that are not too large, for a basic factor is a town's size when walking or cycling is to be encouraged. In addition, it is difficult to transpose travel patterns since all towns have their own characteristics. Thus, even with a strong policy resolve, changes cannot be made from one day to the next.

To start with, policy decisionmakers have to be given empirical data on journeys. It can also be pointed out to them that, since journeys are frequently over short distances, the car is not irreplaceable. What must be stressed is that perceptions of transport modes are sometimes subjective and inaccurate. The private car is not indispensable and can be replaced by more ecological types of transport for a substantial number of journeys. These are the kind of facts which should be highlighted for decisionmakers, prior to the new step of thinking about alternative solutions.

In this context, short-distance mechanised transport can bridge the gaps in transport supply. It is, however, in stations, airports and in any self-contained complex that mechanised transport systems seem more suitable. If the investment is planned in the project design phase, the costs can be internalised. On the other hand, it is more difficult to provide the missing links in the centres of old towns. Objectives on aesthetic grounds will be made, and construction costs cannot be written down. Here the answer will rather be to organise minibus shuttle services.

One factor which may be an obstacle to mechanised transport is the relative technical immaturity of these systems. The limited experience with the systems available and their heterogeneity make it difficult to quantify construction and operating costs for short-distance mechanised transport. Policy decisionmakers may well therefore be loathe to finance such investment. Airports will, however, play a leading role as a logical source of solutions for other fields. Town centres will also be equipped with driverless electric taxis which will be available for tourists and provide a means of ecological short-distance transport.

CONCLUSIONS

The reduction of disamenities caused by car traffic is a major objective in all cities. The policymakers confronted with this task are not completely powerless, and in this area information will play a basic, strategic role, for behavioural changes can be brought about by briefing the public on the alternatives available. The main objective here will be to make better use of public transport.

Other possibilities exist, however, with the ecological modes, i.e. walking and cycling. Since many destination points in towns are not far away it would be possible to walk or cycle to them, even if at present the car is used for such trips. To bring about such a change, it is necessary to win over the following parties:

-- The policymakers, so that decisions will be taken on modifications to promote the safety of infrastructure and its use by ecological transport modes;
-- The planners, who must design compact towns where places of work, dwellings, recreational facilities, local authority offices and shops will be within walking distance;
-- The public, so that, realising what is at stake, they will refrain from using their cars at certain times during the week.

The introduction of an urban infrastructure user charge, varying with the time and day, may be a powerful economic deterrent to the use of the car. It is, in fact, by combining a number of complementary measures that greater and substantial use of ecological modes can be achieved.

Mechanised short-distance transport modes also contribute to public transport and are intended to make up for the lack of services over distances between 500 and 2 000 metres. A wide range of techniques can be considered, from the minibus to the moving pavement. But such a wide choice of systems may pose a problem owing to their lack of technical maturity. This also makes it more difficult to estimate their costs. However, mechanised short-distance transport is ideal for movements in self-contained complexes, such as stations or airports, where there is, moreover, no need for a tariff system.

LIST OF PARTICIPANTS

Professor Maurits VAN WITSEN   **Chairman**
PO Box 19111
NL-3501 DC UTRECHT

Monsieur A. BIEBER   **Rapporteur**
Directeur pour la Prospective
des Transports
INRETS
2 av. du Général Malleret-Joinville
F-94114 ARCUEIL CEDEX

Mr. Werner BRÖG   **Co-Rapporteur**
Managing Director
SOCIALDATA
Postfach 70 16 29
D-8000 MÜNCHEN

Mr. Erhard ERL   **Co-Rapporteur**
SOCIALDATA
Postfach 70 16 29
D-8000 MÜNCHEN

Pr. T. BASIEWICZ
Politechnika Warszawaska
Institut für Transport
ul Koszykowa 75
PL-00662 VARSOVIE

Dr. Tilman BRACHER
IVU - Gesellschaft für Informatif,
Verkehrs- und Umweltplanung
Bundesallee 129
D- 1000 BERLIN 41

Prof. Heinrich BRÄNDLI
Institut für Verkehrsplanung
und Transporttechnik
Hönggerberg
CH-8093 ZÜRICH

Mr. Harri CAVEN
Head of Road Transport Department
Ministry of Transport and Communications
PL 235
SF-00131 HELSINKI 13

Madame Chantal DUCHENE
Centre d'Etudes des Transports Urbains
CETUR
8 avenue Aristide Briand
F-92220 BAGNEUX

Prof. Wolfgang HEINZE
Technische Universität Berlin
Fachgebiet Verkehrswirtschaft und Verkehrspolitik
Alt-Moabit 91c
D-1000 BERLIN 21

Dr. Kjell JANSSON
Department of Economics
Stockholm University
S-10691 STOCKHOLM

Prof. Dr. Hendrik KEERIS
Economische Hogeschool Limburg
Campus Universitaire
B-3610 DIEPENBEEK

Mr. R.H. MEADS
Marketing and Services
Head of Business Planning
London Underground Limited
55 Broadway
GB-LONDON SW1H 0BD

Monsieur José MIRALLES
Departamento de Urbanismo
Universidad Politécnica Valencia
E-46071 VALENCIA

Prof. Ing. Antonio MUSSO
Via d. Cirillo 15
I-00197 ROME

Monsieur Fernando NUNES DA SILVA
CESUR
Instituto Superior Técnico
Av. Rovisco Pais 1
P-1096 LISBONNE CODEX

Monsieur Maurice PIERRON
Chef de la Division Investissements
STP
98 rue de Sèvres
F-75007 PARIS

Dr. Gerd SAMMER
Institut für Strassenbau und Verkehrswesen
Technische Universität Graz
Rechbauerstrasse 12
A-8010 GRAZ

Dr. T. TIELEMAN
Corporate Economics Department
NV Nederlandse Spoorwegen
PO Box 2025
NL-3500 UTRECHT

Dr. Füsun ÜLENGIN
Istanbul Technical University
Faculty of Management
Department of Industrial Engineering
Maçka
TR-80680 ISTANBUL

Drs. G.J. VAN WERVEN
Gemeente Groningen
Afdeling Verkeerszaken
Grote Markt 1
NL-9712 HN GRONINGEN

Mr. Nils Adreas VIBE
Research Sociologist
Department of Transport Planning
Institute of Transport Economics (TOI)
P.O. Box 6110
Etterstad
N-0602 OSLO

Mr. Peter WHITE
Senior Lecturer
University of Westminster
Transport Studies Group
35 Marylebone Road
GB-LONDON NW1 5LS

Mr. C. ZEKKOS
Dromos OEM
Leof. Kifissias 16
MAROUSSI 151 25
GR-ATHENS

ECMT SECRETARIAT

Mr. Gerhard AURBACH
Secretary-General

ECONOMIC RESEARCH AND DOCUMENTATION DIVISION

Mr. Arthur DE WAELE
Head of Division

Mr. Michel VIOLLAND
Administrator

Mrs Paulette COQUAND
Administrator

Ms Françoise ROULLET
Assistant

ALSO AVAILABLE

Possibilities and Limitations of Combined Transport. Series ECMT - Round Table 91 (1993)
(75 93 04 1) ISBN 92-821-1183-0   France FF90   Other Countries FF115   US$21   DM37

Marketing and Service Quality in Public Transport. Series ECMT - Round Table 92 (1993)
(75 93 05 1) ISBN 92-821-1184-9   France FF150 Other Countries FF195   US$34   DM62

Benefits of Different Transport Modes. Series ECMT - Round Table 93 (1994)
(75 94 01 1) ISBN 92-821-1189-X   France FF80   Other Countries FF105   US$18   DM30

Regional Policy, Transport Networks and Communications. Series ECMT - Round Table 94
(1994)
(75 94 04 1) ISBN 92-821-1191-1   France FF100 Other Countries FF130   US$22   DM40

Transport Infrastructure and Systems for a New Europe. Series ECMT - Round Table 95
(1994)
(75 94 06 1) ISBN 92-821-14146-4   France FF110 Other Countries FF140   US$25   DM43

Prices charged at the OECD Bookshop.

The OECD CATALOGUE OF PUBLICATIONS and supplements will be sent free of charge
on request addressed either to OECD Publications Service,
or to the OECD Distributor in your country.

MAIN SALES OUTLETS OF OECD PUBLICATIONS
PRINCIPAUX POINTS DE VENTE DES PUBLICATIONS DE L'OCDE

ARGENTINA – ARGENTINE
Carlos Hirsch S.R.L.
Galería Güemes, Florida 165, 4° Piso
1333 Buenos Aires   Tel. (1) 331.1787 y 331.2391
                     Telefax: (1) 331.1787

AUSTRALIA – AUSTRALIE
D.A. Information Services
648 Whitehorse Road, P.O.B 163
Mitcham, Victoria 3132   Tel. (03) 873.4411
                         Telefax: (03) 873.5679

AUSTRIA – AUTRICHE
Gerold & Co.
Graben 31
Wien I   Tel. (0222) 533.50.14

BELGIUM – BELGIQUE
Jean De Lannoy
Avenue du Roi 202
B-1060 Bruxelles   Tel. (02) 538.51.69/538.08.41
                    Telefax: (02) 538.08.41

CANADA
Renouf Publishing Company Ltd.
1294 Algoma Road
Ottawa, ON K1B 3W8   Tel. (613) 741.4333
                         Telefax: (613) 741.5439
Stores:
61 Sparks Street
Ottawa, ON K1P 5R1   Tel. (613) 238.8985
211 Yonge Street
Toronto, ON M5B 1M4   Tel. (416) 363.3171
                         Telefax: (416)363.59.63
Les Éditions La Liberté Inc.
3020 Chemin Sainte-Foy
Sainte-Foy, PQ G1X 3V6   Tel. (418) 658.3763
                         Telefax: (418) 658.3763

Federal Publications Inc.
165 University Avenue, Suite 701
Toronto, ON M5H 3B8   Tel. (416) 860.1611
                         Telefax: (416) 860.1608
Les Publications Fédérales
1185 Université
Montréal, QC H3B 3A7   Tel. (514) 954.1633
                         Telefax : (514) 954.1635

CHINA – CHINE
China National Publications Import
Export Corporation (CNPIEC)
16 Gongti E. Road, Chaoyang District
P.O. Box 88 or 50
Beijing 100704 PR   Tel. (01) 506.6688
                         Telefax: (01) 506.3101

DENMARK – DANEMARK
Munksgaard Book and Subscription Service
35, Nørre Søgade, P.O. Box 2148
DK-1016 København K   Tel. (33) 12.85.70
                         Telefax: (33) 12.93.87

FINLAND – FINLANDE
Akateeminen Kirjakauppa
Keskuskatu 1, P.O. Box 128
00100 Helsinki
Subscription Services/Agence d'abonnements :
P.O. Box 23
00371 Helsinki   Tel. (358 0) 12141
                         Telefax: (358 0) 121.4450

FRANCE
OECD/OCDE
Mail Orders/Commandes par correspondance:
2, rue André-Pascal
75775 Paris Cedex 16   Tel. (33-1) 45.24.82.00
                        Telefax: (33-1) 49.10.42.76
                        Telex: 640048 OCDE

OECD Bookshop/Librairie de l'OCDE :
33, rue Octave-Feuillet
75016 Paris   Tel. (33-1) 45.24.81.67
                         (33-1) 45.24.81.81
Documentation Française
29, quai Voltaire
75007 Paris   Tel. 40.15.70.00
Gibert Jeune (Droit-Économie)
6, place Saint-Michel
75006 Paris   Tel. 43.25.91.19
Librairie du Commerce International
10, avenue d'Iéna
75016 Paris   Tel. 40.73.34.60
Librairie Dunod
Université Paris-Dauphine
Place du Maréchal de Lattre de Tassigny
75016 Paris   Tel. (1) 44.05.40.13
Librairie Lavoisier
11, rue Lavoisier
75008 Paris   Tel. 42.65.39.95
Librairie L.G.D.J. - Montchrestien
20, rue Soufflot
75005 Paris   Tel. 46.33.89.85
Librairie des Sciences Politiques
30, rue Saint-Guillaume
75007 Paris   Tel. 45.48.36.02
P.U.F.
49, boulevard Saint-Michel
75005 Paris   Tel. 43.25.83.40
Librairie de l'Université
12a, rue Nazareth
13100 Aix-en-Provence   Tel. (16) 42.26.18.08
Documentation Française
165, rue Garibaldi
69003 Lyon   Tel. (16) 78.63.32.23
Librairie Decitre
29, place Bellecour
69002 Lyon   Tel. (16) 72.40.54.54

GERMANY – ALLEMAGNE
OECD Publications and Information Centre
August-Bebel-Allee 6
D-53175 Bonn   Tel. (0228) 959.120
                         Telefax: (0228) 959.12.17

GREECE – GRÈCE
Librairie Kauffmann
Mavrokordatou 9
106 78 Athens   Tel. (01) 32.55.321
                         Telefax: (01) 36.33.967

HONG-KONG
Swindon Book Co. Ltd.
13–15 Lock Road
Kowloon, Hong Kong   Tel. 366.80.31
                         Telefax: 739.49.75

HUNGARY – HONGRIE
Euro Info Service
Margitsziget, Európa Ház
1138 Budapest   Tel. (1) 111.62.16
                         Telefax : (1) 111.60.61

ICELAND – ISLANDE
Mál Mog Menning
Laugavegi 18, Pósthólf 392
121 Reykjavik   Tel. 162.35.23

INDIA – INDE
Oxford Book and Stationery Co.
Scindia House
New Delhi 110001   Tel.(11) 331.5896/5308
                         Telefax: (11) 332.5993
17 Park Street
Calcutta 700016   Tel. 240832

INDONESIA – INDONÉSIE
Pdii-Lipi
P.O. Box 269/JKSMG/88
Jakarta 12790   Tel. 583467
                         Telex: 62 875

ISRAEL
Praedicta
5 Shatner Street
P.O. Box 34030
Jerusalem 91430   Tel. (2) 52.84.90/1/2
                         Telefax: (2) 52.84.93
R.O.Y.
P.O. Box 13056
Tel Aviv 61130   Tél. (3) 49.61.08
                         Telefax (3) 544.60.39

ITALY – ITALIE
Libreria Commissionaria Sansoni
Via Duca di Calabria 1/1
50125 Firenze   Tel. (055) 64.54.15
                         Telefax: (055) 64.12.57
Via Bartolini 29
20155 Milano   Tel. (02) 36.50.83
Editrice e Libreria Herder
Piazza Montecitorio 120
00186 Roma   Tel. 679.46.28
                         Telefax: 678.47.51
Libreria Hoepli
Via Hoepli 5
20121 Milano   Tel. (02) 86.54.46
                         Telefax: (02) 805.28.86
Libreria Scientifica
Dott. Lucio de Biasio 'Aeiou'
Via Coronelli, 6
20146 Milano   Tel. (02) 48.95.45.52
                         Telefax: (02) 48.95.45.48

JAPAN – JAPON
OECD Publications and Information Centre
Landic Akasaka Building
2-3-4 Akasaka, Minato-ku
Tokyo 107   Tel. (81.3) 3586.2016
                         Telefax: (81.3) 3584.7929

KOREA – CORÉE
Kyobo Book Centre Co. Ltd.
P.O. Box 1658, Kwang Hwa Moon
Seoul   Tel. 730.78.91
                         Telefax: 735.00.30

MALAYSIA – MALAISIE
Co-operative Bookshop Ltd.
University of Malaya
P.O. Box 1127, Jalan Pantai Baru
59700 Kuala Lumpur
Malaysia   Tel. 756.5000/756.5425
                         Telefax: 757.3661

MEXICO – MEXIQUE
Revistas y Periodicos Internacionales S.A. de C.V.
Florencia 57 - 1004
Mexico, D.F. 06600   Tel. 207.81.00
                         Telefax : 208.39.79

NETHERLANDS – PAYS-BAS
SDU Uitgeverij Plantijnstraat
Externe Fondsen
Postbus 20014
2500 EA's-Gravenhage   Tel. (070) 37.89.880
Voor bestellingen: Telefax: (070) 34.75.778

NEW ZEALAND
NOUVELLE-ZÉLANDE
Legislation Services
P.O. Box 12418
Thorndon, Wellington   Tel. (04) 496.5652
                         Telefax: (04) 496.5698

NORWAY – NORVÈGE
Narvesen Info Center – NIC
Bertrand Narvesens vei 2
P.O. Box 6125 Etterstad
0602 Oslo 6   Tel. (022) 57.33.00
                              Telefax: (022) 68.19.01

PAKISTAN
Mirza Book Agency
65 Shahrah Quaid-E-Azam
Lahore 54000   Tel. (42) 353.601
                              Telefax: (42) 231.730

PHILIPPINE – PHILIPPINES
International Book Center
5th Floor, Filipinas Life Bldg.
Ayala Avenue
Metro Manila   Tel. 81.96.76
                              Telex 23312 RHP PH

PORTUGAL
Livraria Portugal
Rua do Carmo 70-74
Apart. 2681
1200 Lisboa   Tel.: (01) 347.49.82/5
                          Telefax: (01) 347.02.64

SINGAPORE – SINGAPOUR
Gower Asia Pacific Pte Ltd.
Golden Wheel Building
41, Kallang Pudding Road, No. 04-03
Singapore 1334   Tel. 741.5166
                              Telefax: 742.9356

SPAIN – ESPAGNE
Mundi-Prensa Libros S.A.
Castelló 37, Apartado 1223
Madrid 28001   Tel. (91) 431.33.99
                              Telefax: (91) 575.39.98

Libreria Internacional AEDOS
Consejo de Ciento 391
08009 – Barcelona   Tel. (93) 488.30.09
                              Telefax: (93) 487.76.59
Llibreria de la Generalitat
Palau Moja
Rambla dels Estudis, 118
08002 – Barcelona
              (Subscripcions) Tel. (93) 318.80.12
              (Publicacions) Tel. (93) 302.67.23
                              Telefax: (93) 412.18.54

SRI LANKA
Centre for Policy Research
c/o Colombo Agencies Ltd.
No. 300-304, Galle Road
Colombo 3   Tel. (1) 574240, 573551-2
                   Telefax: (1) 575394, 510711

SWEDEN – SUÈDE
Fritzes Information Center
Box 16356
Regeringsgatan 12
106 47 Stockholm   Tel. (08) 690.90.90
                              Telefax: (08) 20.50.21

Subscription Agency/Agence d'abonnements :
Wennergren-Williams Info AB
P.O. Box 1305
171 25 Solna   Tel. (08) 705.97.50
                              Téléfax : (08) 27.00.71

SWITZERLAND – SUISSE
Maditec S.A. (Books and Periodicals - Livres
et périodiques)
Chemin des Palettes 4
Case postale 266
1020 Renens   Tel. (021) 635.08.65
                              Telefax: (021) 635.07.80

Librairie Payot S.A.
4, place Pépinet
CP 3212
1002 Lausanne   Tel. (021) 341.33.48
                              Telefax: (021) 341.33.45

Librairie Unilivres
6, rue de Candolle
1205 Genève   Tel. (022) 320.26.23
                              Telefax: (022) 329.73.18

Subscription Agency/Agence d'abonnements :
Dynapresse Marketing S.A.
38 avenue Vibert
1227 Carouge   Tel.: (022) 308.07.89
                              Telefax : (022) 308.07.99

See also – Voir aussi :
OECD Publications and Information Centre
August-Bebel-Allee 6
D-53175 Bonn (Germany)   Tel. (0228) 959.120
                         Telefax: (0228) 959.12.17

TAIWAN – FORMOSE
Good Faith Worldwide Int'l. Co. Ltd.
9th Floor, No. 118, Sec. 2
Chung Hsiao E. Road
Taipei   Tel. (02) 391.7396/391.7397
                   Telefax: (02) 394.9176

THAILAND – THAÏLANDE
Suksit Siam Co. Ltd.
113, 115 Fuang Nakhon Rd.
Opp. Wat Rajbopith
Bangkok 10200   Tel. (662) 225.9531/2
                              Telefax: (662) 222.5188

TURKEY – TURQUIE
Kültür Yayinlari Is-Türk Ltd. Sti.
Atatürk Bulvari No. 191/Kat 13
Kavaklidere/Ankara   Tel. 428.11.40 Ext. 2458
Dolmabahce Cad. No. 29
Besiktas/Istanbul   Tel. 260.71.88
                              Telex: 43482B

UNITED KINGDOM – ROYAUME-UNI
HMSO
Gen. enquiries   Tel. (071) 873 0011
Postal orders only:
P.O. Box 276, London SW8 5DT
Personal Callers HMSO Bookshop
49 High Holborn, London WC1V 6HB
                              Telefax: (071) 873 8200
Branches at: Belfast, Birmingham, Bristol, Edin-
burgh, Manchester

UNITED STATES – ÉTATS-UNIS
OECD Publications and Information Centre
2001 L Street N.W., Suite 700
Washington, D.C. 20036-4910 Tel. (202) 785.6323
                           Telefax: (202) 785.0350

VENEZUELA
Libreria del Este
Avda F. Miranda 52, Aptdo. 60337
Edificio Galipán
Caracas 106   Tel. 951.1705/951.2307/951.1297
                Telegram: Libreste Caracas

Subscription to OECD periodicals may also be
placed through main subscription agencies.

Les abonnements aux publications périodiques de
l'OCDE peuvent être souscrits auprès des
principales agences d'abonnement.

Orders and inquiries from countries where Distribu-
tors have not yet been appointed should be sent to:
OECD Publications Service, 2 rue André-Pascal,
75775 Paris Cedex 16, France.

Les commandes provenant de pays où l'OCDE n'a
pas encore désigné de distributeur devraient être
adressées à : OCDE, Service des Publications,
2, rue André-Pascal, 75775 Paris Cedex 16, France.

9-1994

OECD PUBLICATIONS, 2 rue André-Pascal, 75775 PARIS CEDEX 16
PRINTED IN FRANCE
(75 94 09 1) ISBN 92-821-1193-8 - No. 47401 1994

2960 001